POLICY AND PRACTICE IN EL

SERIES EDITORS
JIM O'BRIEN and **CHRISTINE FORDE**

FAMILY LEARNING: ENGAGING WITH PARENTS

Jeannie Mackenzie

*Director, Conditions for Learning and
Convenor of the Scottish Network for
Parental Involvement in Children's Learning*

DUNEDIN

For Andrew and Annie Mackenzie,
from whom I learnt my first and most important lessons

Published by
Dunedin Academic Press Ltd
Hudson House
8 Albany Street
Edinburgh EH1 3QB
Scotland

ISBN 978-1- 903765-99-9
ISSN 1479-6910

British Library Cataloguing in Publication data
A catalogue record for this book is available from the British Library

Typeset by Makar Publishing Production
Printed and bound by CPI Group (UK) Ltd, Croydon, CR0 4YY
Printed on paper from sustainable resources

Contents

Series Editors' Introduction

In a series which examines the connection between policy and practice in education a book examining the relationship between family, home and school is an essential element. Jeannie Mackenzie's book on family learning makes an important contribution to the policy discussions surrounding the relationship between home and school. The idea of family learning is not new in education, but it is undergoing resurgence as the importance of bringing together parents, children and the school to enhance learning is recognised. Jeannie Mackenzie critiques the current policy focus on parental represent-ation in the governance of schools and highlights the limited impact that this approach to parental involvement has on children's learning. Instead, the author argues, we need to appreciate and support the family and the wider community as the context for much rich learning experiences. She demon-strates the possibilities offered by strategies which promote family learning by reconnecting disadvantaged families with education and thus helping to rebuild communities. Though this is a powerful approach to tackling dis-advantage, the author also argues that family learning strategies have the potential to support meaningful learning opportunities for all children and their families.

Dr Jim O'Brien
Professor of Leadership & Professional Learning, Dean and Director, Moray House School of Education, The University of Edinburgh

Christine Forde
Professor of Leadership & Professional Learning, Department of Educational Studies, Faculty of Education, The University of Glasgow

About the Author

Jeannie Mackenzie is Director of an educational consultancy, Conditions for Learning. After 15 years' experience teaching in primary, secondary and special education, she became convinced that if schools were to be more effective, there needed to be a greater engagement with children, young people, the family and the wider community. This conviction led her into pioneering home–school–community work in Port Glasgow and Paisley under the European Urban Aid programme.

Jeannie lectured on equalities at the University of Glasgow and on gender equality and childhood studies for the Open University. She was appointed Integration Manager of the first integrated community schools pilot in East Renfrewshire in 1999. She was Quality Improvement Officer between 2002 and 2007, holding remits for health improvement, parental involvement, community learning and development, family learning and equalities.

Jeannie established Conditions for Learning in 2007, see (www.conditionsforlearning.org). As a social researcher, she has published in the fields of disaffection, parental involvement and classroom relationships. She is a Home School Partnership Adviser for Save the Children, a Trustee of Children 1st, Convener of the Scottish Network for Parental Involvement in Learning and a regular columnist for the *Times Educational Supplement (Scotland)*.

Foreword

There have been many occasions during my professional career when I have longed to be able to lay my hands on a book about family learning.

Working for over 40 years as youth worker, adult educator, education officer, assistant director of education, researcher and professor of community education, I have been concerned with learning in communities and the crucial role of parents in their children's learning. I am not a trained teacher; my professional background is in youth work and community education. Yet the message of this book is as challenging to me as it will be to all involved in school education and everyone who wishes to maximise the educational development of all young people and empower parents as educators.

Jeannie Mackenzie takes us to the heart of territory where the concerns of parents, educators in schools and the community actually meet and where potential joint working and professional collaboration become compelling and a positive invitation to create change. She has assembled convincing international and well-regarded research which draws clear links between parents' involvement in learning relationships with their children, and marked improvement in each child's attainment, confidence and progression within school. Similar evidence is presented which demonstrates the significant effect which an acknowledged and nurtured parental educational role can have upon the confidence and personal development of parents and other adult relatives. Family learning is shown to be a creator of social capital because these benefits spread within both school and community.

The author has taught in primary and secondary schools; worked in community-based educational projects in disadvantaged communities and latterly served as a quality improvement officer in an education authority. As a result, her research on the current practice of family learning in Scotland is authoritative, instructive and reveals the non-statutory and somewhat patchy nature of local authority provision. Case studies that outline the contrasting characteristics of current practice and the advantages and challenges of this kind of work are invaluable as a guide to other teachers, field workers and researchers who will wish to examine the varied approaches and outcomes. The comprehensive chapter on definitions of family learning will serve to clarify what is and what is not family learning, and should provoke a further debate about progress and development.

Usually, books which are concerned with the exposition and teasing out of concepts, the presentation of contrasting research, the examination of theory and practice and the presentation of political and theoretical arguments for the mainstream adoption of an educational idea, do not dip into the 'How to do it' and 'How will we know when it is done well?'. Perhaps the reason for this is that theoretical writers do not always have the experience on the ground. This book is different and gives a comprehensive perspective on ways in which objectives for family learning can be developed and how practice can be assessed using a range of techniques and methods.

So, why do I wish I had been able to lay my hands on this book during my career? It is because the book takes the reader on a journey from definition to delivery and evaluation, through the exploration of educational context and the relationship of theory to practice. It is also because of the way it is open about values, the reiteration of the importance of parents to a child's learning; the challenge to provide family learning as an integral part of educational services and the need for professional change.

Ted Milburn CBE
Emeritus Professor
The University of Strathclyde
Formerly Professor of Education and Director of the Scottish Research
Centre for Youth Work Studies, The University of Strathclyde

Introduction

Children are educated by their whole environment ...
the school has a specialist function, but the central
place belongs to the family. *(Grant, 1989, p. 126)*

Across Scotland, there is a wide range of work with parents carried out by schools and other agencies. Since the passing of the Scottish Schools (Parental Involvement Act) in 2006, there has been a renewed interest in working with parents, accompanied by concerns that while the legislation may increase the number of parents active in schools, it may be less effectual in increasing the genuine involvement of parents in their children's learning. This book explores the history of promoting parental involvement in learning in Scotland since the 1970s and its connection with international developments in that arena. It seeks to clarify the range of terms used. It contends that in seeking to increase parental involvement in learning, schools are liable to use means that are informed by the professional expertise of teachers, thus unintentionally distancing, disengaging and disempowering the very parents schools most wish to reach. This practice is contrasted with that of family learning, which uses an appreciative, affirming and accessible approach to achieve the goal. The book proposes a working definition of family learning and means to measure its effectiveness. Family learning is located within social and situational theories of learning and the reader is provided with practical examples from across Scotland. Finally, some practical suggestions are made for establishing family learning as a mainstream educational approach.

To understand the concept of family learning, it is useful to consider its roots in the educational movements of the 1970s, as educators responded to research findings that challenged existing beliefs and understandings of how children learn. One of the most significant of these challenges was to the theories of Jean Piaget, who postulated a linear development of children's thought, with clearly differentiated phases. Piagets's theories were based on experimentation which appeared to reveal that young children could not, for example, conceive how an object would look different from another person's point of view. These theories were challenged by Martin Hughes and others, who found the children had simply not understood Piaget's instructions, but could understand when the experiments were described to them in a way that made sense to their lives, when language was used that revealed their potential (Donaldson, 1978, pp. 19–25). Barbara Tizard was influential at the same time in revealing the false inferences that can be made about the child's home environment and the extent to which they have acquired language. She was also seminal in her illumination of the power of the learning environment in the home and in casting doubt on professional perceptions about the lack of learning opportunities in working-class homes (Tizard, 1975, pp. 17–33). Most influential to the growth of family learning was the writing of Paulo Freire, and in particular his conviction that every human being is capable of looking critically at the world in a dialogical encounter with others (Freire, 1970, p. 14). These three sets of challenges to the thinking of the time encapsulate the values that underpin family learning: that is, parents as educators, language as power and education as dialogue. The way these new understandings affected practice are best understood in examining how these values were to underpin the work of one of foremost practitioners in family learning in Scotland, Doreen Grant.

1974 was a landmark year in the history of parental involvement in Scottish education. In that year, Sister Doreen Grant began an investigative piece of work with parents in a run down housing estate in Govan, Glasgow (Grant, 1989, p. 1). As a teacher, Grant had become frustrated by the persistent failure of schools serving areas of poverty to achieve successful educational outcomes for pupils. The received wisdom of her day was that the best predictor of academic achievement was a pupil's home address. We now know that this is not so – in fact the best predictor of academic success in the early years is understood to be the extent of parental involvement in the child's learning (Desforges and Abouchaar, 2003, p. 17; Coleman, 1998, p. 155).

Grant hypothesised that the reason working-class children failed lay in the very different ways in which home and school approached and understood the process of learning. The account of her reflective practice in Govan, and the conclusions she reached, are startlingly fresh and relevant for today. She not only proposed a genuine partnership in learning between home and school, but she also demonstrated how this could be achieved. The significance of Grant's work lies not in this recognition alone, but in the strong theoretical foundation from which she derived the three values that guided the project. These, as we have already seen, are the value of parents as educators, the acknowledgement that language is power and the central position of dialogue in education.

The revolutionary nature of the approach is seen in how these values challenged not only the assumptions on which much work with parents was carried out at the time, but also the power differential which existed, and still exists, between home and school.

Parents as educators

In the 1970s, although there was a growing recognition of the importance of parental involvement (Grant, 1989, p. 127), valuing the role of parents as educators still ran counter to the dominant view. Parents were too often regarded as part of the problem of underachievement, rather than part of the solution. Parents were expected to play minor roles, ensuring their children attended school, completed homework and behaved appropriately. The value of learning in the home was underrated and sometimes seen as running counter to the value of school education. It was common in the 1970s, for example, for teachers to tell parents not to teach children letters, in case they taught them 'the wrong way'. Education was seen as compensatory, making up for the poor start in life that these children's homes offered, contrasting with Grant's vision of the parent as co-educator. The roles parents are now expected to play in Scottish education are much broader, as discussed in Chapter 2.

Language as power

The development of language in young children gives them the ability to analyse and to synthesise objects and behaviours in the world they observe. A code develops which enables children to unlock their potential for learning. It also gives them the power to communicate needs, feelings and thoughts. As a child develops language, there is a step change in the speed with which they learn about the world. However, language alone is not enough; it must aid children in organising their thought through interacting verbally with adults (Grant, 1989, p. 130). In the closed world of the classroom, much learning necessarily depends on the use of language. Grant observed in her teaching that many working-class children did not readily respond to teacher questioning. Yet these were children who had well developed language that they used in their home and community. What dissuaded them from entering into dialogue with their teacher was the apparent divergence of the code between home and school. At home and play, the children used speech patterns that suited their immediate context, while at school they were addressed in speech patterns that did not depend on context. The language used in school was the language of power, described as 'talking properly'. Bernstein termed these forms of speech 'restricted' and 'elaborate', but has since been criticised for the crude distinctions of class and lack of empirical data confirming the thesis (Fulcher and Scott, 1999, pp. 234–5). Most writers agree the phenomenon exists, but different explanations are given. For example, Labov suggested that the notion of working-class children's verbal deprivation exists because working-class children became monosyllabic when questioned by middle-class professionals (Tizard and Hughes, 2002, p. 110). Whatever the explanation, the failure of professionals to acknowledge and value the language spoken by the children has historically contributed to the poor school performance of many children living in poverty. Grant explored the answer to this cultural diversity through the development of what was to be later known as 'mutual learning cultures': that is, cultures that encourage the sharing of the understanding of how we name and comprehend our world.

Education as dialogue

Instead of a teacher–parent communication limited to professionals providing information, Grant proposed an approach to conversations between home and school based on the work of Paulo Freire (Freire, 1970). The traditional mode of conversations between teacher and parent is one of direction, instruction, guidance and persuasion. Although the language used may be one of partnership, the body language can convey a very different message, and where the spoken and the body language conflict, it is the body language that is believed. Traditional exchanges, based as they often are on curriculum expertise and educational terminology, can be used by teachers to silence the parent. The knowledge that the teacher holds is assumed complete – they are not only free to pronounce on the pupil's progress in learning, but also on their conduct. Yet knowledge, explains Freire, is always incomplete, and questioning and searching are indispensable to learning (Roberts, 2000, p. 146). Where the parent–teacher dyad (or indeed the pupil–teacher–parent triad) is regarded as a learning opportunity for all parties, then a much more powerful communication takes place, and the opportunity for learning is greatly enhanced. Engaging in such dialogue depends on those involved approaching the task both with humility and with hope. Humility is required because without an acceptance that there is always something more to learn in every situation, our minds are closed to new information. Hope is essential to open the mind to the possibility that change can take place, that things can be better, that everyone has something to offer and something to gain from engaging in dialogue. Yet for families living with poverty, disability and social exclusion, hope is a rare commodity. It requires skill on the educator's part to elicit hope. Yet education, of all the public services, is the one uniquely placed to provide hope, offering a possible route out of poverty, oppression and despair.

Education is dynamically developed when parents and professionals carry out this search in partnership. 'Knowledge emerges,' according to Freire, 'through the restless, impatient, continuing, hopeful inquiry people pursue.' Through dialogue, Freire believes, 'people achieve significance as people' (Grant, 1989, p. 131).

Partnership with Parents, Strathclyde Region

Partnership with parents in Scotland received a major boost in the 1980s, when Strathclyde Region (at that time the largest local authority in Europe) established the Partnership with Parents Project, with Doreen Grant serving as the first project leader. The project was partially funded by the Van Leer Foundation, and it drew inspiration from the Head Start programmes in the USA, and from the writings of Paulo Freire, Margaret Donaldson and Barbara Tizard (Orton, 1991, pp. 8–12). Orton outlines the project's principles as:

- valuing others;
- experience-based learning;
- providing opportunities for interactive language;
- using the plan/act/reflect cycle of learning; and
- collaboration. (Orton, 1991)

Orton outlined how each of these values was based on the theoretical work of Freire, Donaldson and Tizard, and the implications for professionals who espouse these values. As these theoretical foundations are central to family learning, I have expanded on Orton's analysis, related it more directly to family learning and sought below to make it relevant for today.

Freire valued people as active in their learning, not as passive recipients of knowledge. He contrasted the 'banking' system of education (where the learner is seen as a vault into which the teacher 'deposits' facts) with a learning experience that encourages both teacher and learner to engage in dialogue and to learn from one another (Freire, 1970, pp. 52–67). He contrasts the humanist educator with the 'anti-dialogical banking educators' who approach the learners with projects which may correspond to the educators' view of the world, but not to the learners' perspective (Freire, 1970, pp. 74–5). The implication of Freire's approach for the professional role with families is that they will value not only what the learner brings to the learning, but will value the learner's views on what should be learned and how it should be learned. The professionals will not impose their own values about learning, but rather seek to involve the learner in sharing their values and concerns. This thinking is at the heart of learner-centred approaches such as personal learning planning (Scottish Office, 1998) and in the type of family learning programme which encourages the growth of parent groups that form to achieve specific aims they have identified for themselves.

Believing in experience-based learning, Freire rejected the use textbooks in his adult teaching – rather he worked from the words that people used and explored the meaning of these words in a social context that was significant for the learners. He situated educational activity in the lived experience of participants, rather than in a formal curriculum (Freire, 1970, p. 69). Donaldson emphasised that learning begins with situations that are meaningful to the learner, that connect with their understanding of the world (Donaldson, 1978, p. 24). Tizard regarded the familiar and shared contact of parent and child as a rich opportunity for talking, negotiating and learning (Tizard, 1975, pp. 28–33). The message for the professional educator working with families is that the topics for conversations between professionals and parents are not predetermined. Professionals cannot assume that they know what is important to parents in relation to their child's learning. When families experience an activity together, the opportunity to learn for both age groups is embedded in the activity. This thinking informs the type of family learning programme where families experience an activity which they have planned together and the adults afterwards discuss what happened, finding the words and phrases to describe what the experience meant for them and their families. A example of this approach can be found in Chapter 5.

People need time, space and social relationships in order to explore and investigate their world. The small group experience permits interaction and growth, for the educator as well as the educated (Freire, 1970, pp. 69–70). Tizard found that the home was an ideal setting for the type of interactive association on which the learning of young children depends, but which is not so prevalent in the nursery class (Tizard, 1975, pp. 28–33). For the professional working with families, there is no quick fix in partnership with parents – professionals are prepared to invest time to build relationships and to provide space for discussion. Family learning will therefore often take place in small group and in informal contexts, facilitating the building of the relationships.

Freire placed importance on people's consciousness of learning and change, aided by being involved in planning, acting and reflecting. Donaldson valued the plan, act and reflect cycle as a vehicle for developing 'disembedded' thought from the concrete to the abstract (Donaldson, 1978, pp. 76–9). Tizard argued for more dialogue with nursery children, to maximise what they were learning from activity (Tizard, 1975, p. 13). The implications for work with parents is that they should be invited to join in planning activities when they and their children take part, and then be encouraged to reflect on the experience. Learning experiences should be planned with time and space for dialogue about what is being learned.

In Freire's philosophy, teachers and learners are 'co-investigators' engaging in dialogue (Freire, 1970, p. 62). Donaldson stressed the importance of a supportive environment for the young learner, where both at home and in school the child engages in collaborative practices that extend their learning (Donaldson, 1978, p. 94). Tizard argued for a greater sharing between home and school (Tizard, 1975, p. 13). Professionals engage with parents in investigating a topic by taking a step back and viewing the topic afresh. The consequence for professionals is that they regard themselves as collaborating with parents to support children's learning. Parents and professionals work closely together to maximise the potential of both home learning and school learning. An example from family learning is the type of activity when a group of parents wish to investigate an issue that is important for them, and are supported to do so by a professional who has no preconceived notion of what the outcomes will be.

It is the major thesis of this book that the theoretical basis of Grant's work is still relevant today. In 2004, the Scottish Executive published *A Curriculum for Excellence* – a new curriculum for Scottish schools and the early years. Among the drivers to create the new curriculum are the pace of technological change, the threat of environmental instability and the need for Scottish children to acquire the knowledge, skills and attributes for the future. They need to be equipped to solve problems we cannot yet conceive, create new knowledge at a speed we can only imagine and be able to learn co-operatively across social and national boundaries (Scottish Executive, 2004). Other motivations for devising the new curriculum include the continuing gap in achievement associated with poverty and deprivation (OECD, 2007; HMIe, 2007a). These concerns resonate with Freire's distinction between a 'banking education' and a 'problem solving education' as he regards banking education as suppressing criticism and questioning, denying the value of experience in the learning process and treating reality and knowledge as static, thus and hindering the consideration of alternative ways of understanding and solving the world's problems (Roberts, 2005, p. 448). They also chime with Freire's concerns with education's potential to perpetuate inequality (Freire, 1970, p. 59).

Although the theoretical basis of Grant's work is still relevant today, the lessons learned have been only partially applied in Scotland. When funding for the Partnership in Education Project ended in 1996, attempts were made to disseminate the learning throughout the large area that was then Strathclyde Region and beyond. In spite of the success of the approaches used in engaging with parents, the Project failed to gain long lasting support from the key agencies that were involved – school education, community education, libraries and health. While much of the success of the developments lay in the productive relationships established between agencies working in the local areas, this commitment was rarely matched at the strategic level. The reluctance to embrace such learning is not unique to Scotland; similar outcomes have been experienced in British Columbia (Coleman, 1998, p. 160). Despite many years of research, the power of collaboration between families and schools remains unappreciated by many of those concerned with school improvement (Coleman, 1998, p. 160; Vincent, 1996, p. 149). The research and the theoretical basis has been at best misunderstood, and at worst dismissed. Action in parental partnership in education has become a goal of itself, without the benefit of theoretical understandings. Praxis has lost out to practice.

Although 'partnership with parents' is now regarded as a universal good, many schools in Scotland have yet to engage successfully all parents in the authentic partnership that Grant proposed. Grant's guiding values and the Partnership in Education Project's principles have not been universally adopted, and indeed may not have fully been accepted. Scotland is not alone in struggling to achieve partnership with parents; a recent critique of family–school relationships in the United States reveals that a fundamental inequity still frustrates home school partnership and that the power differential between home and school is still overlooked (De Carvalho, 2001, p. 132). The Organisation of Economic Co-operation (OECD) found a similar gap between rhetoric and reality in Canada, England and Wales, France, Germany, Ireland, Japan, Spain and the United States, with Denmark being a notable exception (OECD, 1997, p. 36). Chapters 1 and 2 explore these theoretical issues in more depth.

Taking on board the lessons from the Partners with Parents project demands that schools not only work differently, but also change from a culture that

unwittingly creates distance between home and school. Re-culturing is difficult and it is all too tempting to retreat into restructuring as an easy alternative.
Structures for partnership with parents have long been in place, and these have
been strengthened recently by the Scottish Schools (Parental Involvement) Act
(2006). Resources have been designed and disseminated, specialist posts have
been created and projects have been established. In 1999, the Scottish Executive identified 'engagement with parents' as a key characteristic of the 'new
community schools' (later known as integrated community schools). None
of the structural changes has fully supported the values of family learning
outlined above. However, the increasingly popular concept of building social
capital offers a new vehicle for re-examining these values, and this is explored
in Chapter 4.

In an age of accountability, partnership with parents has lacked credibility,
as there has yet to be developed a means of assuring the quality of the partnership. Although 'partnership with parents' has existed as a quality indicator
in all three editions of *How Good is Our School?*, Her Majesty's Inspectorate
for Education's (HMIe) blueprint for self-evaluation (HMIe, 1992, 2002 and
2007a) the partnership is consistently defined in terms of the school's agenda.
No national measure has yet been devised for assessing how good schools are
at promoting parents' involvement in their children's learning. Some models
for evaluating practice are therefore discussed in Chapter 5.

Much has been achieved, and across Scotland there are examples of excellent practice, some of which are discussed in Chapter 3. However, throughout
the country, and in particular in the areas of most socio-economic deprivation,
there is huge frustration in schools. It is common to hear teaching staff talking
of low turnouts at curriculum workshops, of 'apathetic parents' and of a 'lack
of any genuine involvement'. While excellent practice exists, family learning
is not a mainstream part of our universal services, as discussed in Chapter 6.
Whatever schools are selling, some parents are not buying it. We need, not a
new approach, but rather to refurbish an existing one, and to bring it out of
the shadows and into the forefront of our thinking about school education in
Scotland. This approach is called family learning.

CHAPTER 1

Defining family learning

Learning is inherent in human nature: it is an ongoing and integral part of our lives, not a special kind of activity separable for the rest of our lives. *(Wenger, 1998, p. 226)*

The range of parental involvement work carried out across Scotland has not always been clearly defined. Some of the terms used to describe such work are used interchangeably, and professionals may have a role in more than one type of work with parents and families. The terms in most common use are 'parental involvement', 'partnership with parents', 'family support' and 'family learning'. This chapter describes and critically evaluates these terms. Finally, it proposes a working definition of family learning based on the values outlined in the Introduction: that is, the appreciation of the role of parents as educators, the acknowledgement of language as power and the crucial importance of dialogue in education.

Parental involvement

In his foreword to the Guidance on the Scottish School (Parental Involvement) Act, 2006, Peter Peacock, then Minister for Education, provided a definition of parental involvement: 'Parental involvement is supporting pupils and their learning. It is about parents and teachers working together in partnership to help children become more confident learners' (Scottish Executive, 2006b, p. i).

As we have already seen, the Act placed new duties on schools to promote partnership with parents and parental involvement in children's learning, and the Guidance to the Act defined three areas for parental involvement in schools and learning (Scottish Executive, 2006a, pp. 6–7). However, in spite of three aspects of involvement being identified, little attention is given to the first, which is the involvement of learning at home. Indeed, learning at home is regarded in the Guidance as largely dependent on information and support from the school, rather than as something to be valued in its own right. The Act places duties on schools to provide information and support, but it is not specific about how this can be done in order to engage successfully with all parents. The Guidance to the Act provides some ideas on how to consult with parents, but no detail on methods of engaging with parents who may feel less confident in working with the school. It does not refer to family learning. However, the guidance does identify some barriers to parents becoming involved, including parents' own negative experience of school education, communication that does not take into account literacy needs, cultural diversity and challenging family circumstances. It recommends closer working with other agencies which work with families, and particular efforts to involve fathers.

One of the reasons so little attention is paid within the Guidance to practical means of engaging with parents is that the Act itself, and the surrounding documentation, is overly absorbed with one aspect of parental involvement, which is parent representation through the new parent councils. The role of the parent as consumer occupies more space than other roles that parents may play, and this is disappointing, given that what we now know of the value of parental involvement in children's learning, as opposed to parental involvement in the life of schools or in the management of schools. A major review of the research into parental involvement was carried out on behalf of the Department for Education and Skills (DfES) in England in 2003. The involvement of parents in governance was not found to be significant in improving children's learning – instead parental involvement with learning in the home was found to have the most impact on children's achievement and adjustment (Desforges and Abouchaar, 2003, pp. 4–5). Notions of parental involvement in governance are perennially attractive to policy makers because they create a form of public relations which provide greater institutional legitimacy for current educational practices (Anderson, 1998, p. 573). This can be seen in the recent change in legislation in Scotland, which, while replacing the heavily prescriptive School Boards with more flexible Parent Councils, still clung to governance as the central element of the legislation (Scottish Executive, 2006b). Formal arrangements for governance are popular because they are highly visible and easily quantifiable. It is one of the peculiarities of parental involvement that the most highly visible types have least impact on learning. Learning in the home and in the community has most impact, but it is the least visible and most challenging to measure:

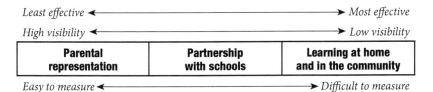

Least effective ◄——————————————————————————► Most effective

High visibility ◄——————————————————————————► Low visibility

Parental representation	Partnership with schools	Learning at home and in the community

Easy to measure ◄——————————————————————► Difficult to measure

Some might argue that schools can have little impact on learning in the home, so must therefore concentrate on the aspects of parental involvement they can influence; however, the DfES report concluded that schools do indeed have the capacity to increase parental involvement in learning in the home (Desforges and Abouchaar, 2003, pp. 4–5). It is possible, if the right approaches are taken, to encourage parents and children to work and learn together in ways that are significant for the educational outcomes of the children.

The 2006 Act was a lost opportunity for Scotland's schooling system to wake up to a more hopeful perspective on how families can strengthen children's learning, ignoring as it did the promotion of more effective forms of parental involvement. This contrasts with the school improvement strategy in England, where support for family learning is set out in the key white paper *Excellence in Schools* (DfEE, 1997) and supported across England and Wales by the National Institute of Adult and Continuing Education (NIACE) which provides a strong research and development lead. In Scotland, our national legislation and policies are currently limited to an understanding of parental involvement as parents supporting the curriculum and taking a role in governance, rather than contributing to a broader meaning of learning which draws on the richness and diversity of families' educational contributions.

Family support

The use of the term 'family support' in connection with schools grew partly out of the integrated community schools initiative (Scottish Executive, 1998). One of the key achievements of the pilot phase of the initiative was increased support for the most vulnerable children and families (Scottish Executive, 2003). Family support tends to focus on supporting parents with issues such as mental health, poverty, disability and other factors which may lead to them finding it difficult to support fully their child's learning. Family support also seeks to develop parenting skills, to improve behaviour, to promote health and to encourage school attendance. There is some evidence that successful interventions in family support can positively influence children's learning (Midlothian Council, 2008), however, like family learning, family support is not mandatory, and it depends on local vision and commitment. Professionals involved in family learning are often also expected to provide family support. It may seem an obvious linking of tasks; however, there is tension between the two responsibilities due to the potential for role confusion and distraction from the principal undertaking. On the other hand, family support at its most effective can ease families into family learning. Parents who face tough issues, such as poverty, homelessness, addictions, chronic illness and domestic abuse can lead lives dominated by these problems, leaving little mental or emotional energy for the children, and even less for their learning. Providing support with these issues can mean that a parent has the freedom to engage with their child's learning for the first time (Midlothian Council, 2008).

Family learning

Family learning emerged in the 1960s as a method of promoting parental involvement in learning in the home. The poor relation of mainstream school education, it has often depended on short-term funding. In many cases, it has been located within the community education sector (now known as community learning and development in Scotland). It has not had a high profile within descriptions of parental involvement in schools. Perhaps more importantly it has never been clearly defined within the school sector; the definitions that exist in the UK have been written within the life-long learning sector (Learning and Skills Council, 2002, p. 1). It has received a great deal of interest and support in England since the publication of *Excellence in Schools* (DfEE, 1997). While there is extensive academic literature on partnership with parents and parental involvement, little has been written on the topic of family learning, in Scotland or elsewhere. The reason for the silence on family learning is that it is often hidden within more accessible concepts such as parental involvement, family literacy or adult learning. Exceptions are the pamphlets and toolkits published by NIACE, which focus on practical advice to practitioners (Lochrie, 2004; Haggart, 2000, 2001). A number of UK groups, including the Scottish Council Foundation, have contributed to a short pamphlet entitled *A Manifesto for Family Learning* which outlines some recommendations for government departments (NIACE, 2000).

Family learning is recognised within the Early Years Framework, which proposes 'developing a culture of community and family learning' (Scottish Government, 2008, pp. 5–7). However, the Framework regards family learning mainly in the context of parenting skills and involvement in the formal education of children. Although the Framework espouses notions of community empowerment and action, there is no clear guidance on how agencies can promote family learning in other contexts, and the document tends to conflate family learning with family support.

Approaches to learning

In seeking to define family learning, I first want to consider how it is situated within a humanist and situational approach to learning, rather than within more traditional behaviourist and cognitivist approaches. Viewed from the formal learning perspective of the school, family learning activity can be misunderstood as merely recreational if the observer is not aware of the approaches informing the practice and how these are embedded in the underpinning values of family learning.

Behaviourist approaches regard the learning process as an observable change in behaviour in response to stimulus. Learning is understood to take place because the learner associates rewards with particular actions. The educator's role is therefore to arrange the learning environment in such a way that it produces the desired response. Praise, the achievement of a good grade in a test, or a feeling of increased accomplishment or satisfaction can all act to reinforce the desired response (Merriman *et al.*, 2007, pp. 278–81).

Cognitivist approaches focus on internal mental processes. Learners are understood to integrate new knowledge with existing understanding as proposed by Piaget (Merriman *et al.*, 2007, p. 285), recommending courses of study where general principles are first introduced, with more detailed and specific matter being provided later and related to the first learning – the 'spiral curriculum' that is now familiar in our schools (Bruner, 1977, p. 13). The cognitivist approach suggests that the role of the educator is to structure the content of the learning so that the learner develops the capacity to think and learn more effectively (Merriman *et al.*, 2007, pp. 284–7).

Parental involvement practice based on underlying behaviourist and cognitivist assumptions will tend to structure the learning environment for parents with set objectives and seek to reinforce desired responses. For example, many schools are now welcoming parents into classrooms with the clear objectives of helping parents to understand the concept of active learning. The desired response is that parents will have the knowledge to support the curriculum and reinforce school learning in the home. The success of these programmes will be evaluated by the extent to which pupil learning and parental co-operation has improved.

In contrast, family learning derives largely from humanist and social/situational approaches to learning, as these are more sympathetic to the underpinning values already established: that is, the appreciation of the role of parents as educators, the acknowledgement that language is power and the central position of dialogue in education.

Humanist approaches to learning assume that learners are motivated to achieve their potential, but that the motivation to learn and to achieve can be subordinate to other more basic needs such as hunger, thirst or physical safety (Merriman *et al.*, 2007, p. 282). This has resonance for promoting family learning; the assumption of the family learning practitioner is that parents are not only keen but also able educators of their children, but that in some cases, more immediate concerns such as poverty and domestic abuse detract from the higher order needs.

The humanist approach is also concerned with learning that leads to personal growth and development, which Carl Rogers characterised as:

- involving the feelings and thinking of the learner;
- being initiated by the learner;
- influencing not only the behaviours but also the attitudes and personality of the learner;
- evaluated by the learner;
- incorporating its meaning into the total experience of the learner.
  (Merriman *et al.*, 2007, p. 282)

It is in the negotiation implicit in the approach that Grant's notion of 'mutual learning cultures' are developed, as the educator and the learner share understanding of how they name and comprehend the world that is of immediate concern to the learner. Opportunities for learners to define learning outcomes for themselves help them acquire more elaborated codes to express challenges and achievements.

The final approach to learning on which family learning is based is situated learning, first proposed by Jean Lave and Etienne Wenger as taking place within 'communities of practice' (Wenger, 1998, p. 12). Wenger takes the perspective that learning is an integral part of our lives and does not necessarily take place within a specialist setting or structure. He regards it as experiential, involving negotiation and engagement with others. This is not to say that it requires no structure; he believes it needs just enough structure so that experience is accumulated and just enough discontinuity so that those involved are continually renegotiating meaning (Wenger, 1998, pp. 226–7). Within the family learning context, examples of this type of learning in practice are provided in Tizard and Hughes' transcripts of parents talking with their four-year-old children during their everyday lives and play. In these sessions, the children initiated discussions in order to satisfy their persistent intellectual curiosity, while parents provided a 'scaffold' for the conversation (Bruner, 1978, p. 19) supporting the children's imagination and negotiating, while also providing boundaries and bridges between concepts (Tizard and Hughes, 2002, pp. 212–13). The value of these learning conversations is contrasted with the limited conversations the same children had with nursery staff, believed to be due to the higher child/adult ratio in the nursery and the lack of participation of nursery staff in the lives of children outside the nursery. Parents were able to elicit a greater depth of learning because they knew their child more intimately and the learning was situated in the child's life and accumulated knowledge (Tizard and Hughes, 2002, p. 222). Tizard and Hughes were recording these conversations in the 1980s. Pre-5 centres and schools are now much more aware of the power of situated learning and much work has been done in the last two decades to bridge the experience of home and school. The *Curriculum for Excellence* offers new opportunities to take on board the concept of situated learning through developing communities of practice within the school, where children and young people can co-operate, be active in their learning, engage in more experiential and social activity and negotiate new meaning as they solve problems together. However, due to the necessarily more formal nature of schooling, there remains an essential difference between the types of learning in the home and the school.

At its core, family learning is about normal family activities that involve at least one adult and one child in an action which creates learning. Enjoying a book, taking a walk, visiting the Post Office, baking a cake, fixing a puncture and playing a computer game all provide contexts for family learning. However, the context itself is not sufficient. For learning to take place, dialogue is essential. The ceaseless questioning of young children and the skill of parental response are critical to the learning that takes place. As the child questions and learns to name objects and their behaviour, he or she is able to unlock new possibilities and new lines of inquiry. It would be wrong, however, to imagine that parents need formal training in how to scaffold the learning. It appears to come naturally, although parents vary greatly in their skill to provide this support. The most effective scaffolding is provided by parents who provide just enough challenge to stretch the child's learning without exposing it to too much failure (Thornton, 2002, pp. 164–6). The reasons for the variation in skill are not clear, however. Tizard and Hughes found no correlation between this ability and social class (Tizard and Hughes, 2002, pp. 109–11), challenging one of the common myths about parental involvement in learning, explored in more detail in Chapter 2.

Most families engage in family learning every day without being self-consciously aware of the process. Indeed, the fluid nature of much family learning is its strength – it is led by the immediate needs and interests of the family members, and it serves a clearly understood purpose. Moreover, it is largely initiated by the child rather than structured by the parent (Tizard and Hughes, 2002, p. 212). That such activity successfully facilitates learning can be demonstrated if we list some of the learning children have overtaken in their first years before formal learning takes place. These include speech, toilet training, tying shoelaces, feeding themselves, mapping their immediate environment, understanding roles and occupations, the use of money, naming and counting objects and understanding that a book is read from left to right.

Although family learning is a normal, everyday activity for most families, professional interest in promoting family learning arises when it is understood that maximizing the potential of family learning can assist children's learning in the more formal setting of pre-school and school. Dialogue is an essential component of learning, and therefore of family learning. In talking about how learning takes place, participants become more confident about their own potential to support their children's learning, and may begin to articulate aspirations for their own learning (Grant, 1989, p. 130). A family learning activity will often result in a product that enhances the community, perhaps a musical or dramatic production, a festival, or story-telling event. For example, one group of parents in East Renfrewshire worked with a facilitator to devise a 'word walk' booklet, which families could use to walk around the local environment, encouraging the children to look at 'environmental print': that is, language to be found on street signs, shops windows and the like. The booklet became a local resource available from the public library (East Renfrewshire Council, 2008, p. 20).

Defining family learning

The National Family Learning Network (a UK organisation hosted by the Campaign for Learning), defines family learning as being 'about families enjoying learning together' with key distinctive features including:

- encouraging family members to learn together;
- parents / carers and children learning together;
- parents / carers learning separately in order to engage in learning with children or other family members; and

- children learning separately in order to share learning with other family members. (Campaign for Learning, 2008)

The National Advisory Group for Continuing Education and Lifelong Learning (NAGCELL), a UK organisation, identified the following types of family learning:

- learning concerned with families themselves, their development, internal roles and relationships, parenting, caring, support for children with special needs, bereavement etc.;
- learning focused on the personal learning and other needs of different family members, often as a precursor or preparation for the previous type;
- learning which gives opportunities for two or more family members to learn separately about a common topic or theme, or with a common focus;
- learning which brings together two or more family members to learn together around a common topic, theme or focus;
- learning which is characterised by development, advancement or progression, often building explicitly on other forms of family learning and frequently focused on challenging issues or objectives. (NAGCELL, 1998)

The definition of family learning adopted by HMIe is the one used by the UK national Learning and Skills Council (LSC). The LSC states that family programmes are those which 'aim to encourage family members to learn together. They are learning as or within a family. They should include opportunities for intergenerational learning and, wherever possible, lead both adults and children to pursue further learning' (Learning and Skills Council, 2002, p. 1).

In this book, I propose a definition of family learning which builds on these definitions, by incorporating the three values which were central to Grant's original vision outlined in Chapter 1: that is, parents as educators, language as power and education as dialogue:

> Family learning involves families enjoying learning together. Those who seek to promote family learning acknowledge the central role of the family in a child's learning, validate the nature of that learning by engaging families in dialogue about learning, and facilitate the participation of families in the design and enjoyment of learning.

The promotion of family learning in Scotland has focused almost entirely on areas of social disadvantage, which is understandable given the limited resource available. However, there is good reason to consider it in a wider context. The nature of the family is changing, with many more people than in the past experiencing a number of different family formations and family transitions throughout their lives. For children of working parents, opportunities for family fun and learning may be limited. There is a huge range of out-of-school activities on offer to the children of parents, further fragmenting family life. Opportunities for families to sit down together for a meal, go on an outing together or simply play a game together are becoming rarer due to the pressures of our current lifestyles, with the dominance of age-specific activities, the all pervading electronic media and the increasing pressure of parents' working lives.

CHAPTER 2

Home–school relations

Discussions of parent involvement are full of complexity, competing demands, and struggles over power. *(Lewis and Forman, 2002 p. 84)*

Having outlined the history of family learning in Scotland and proposed a definition, I now seek to explore the nature of relations between home and school and how this affects the promotion of family learning. The discussion is illustrated by a series of personal reflections which take a critical look at my experiences as a parent, practitioner and manager in the field of parental involvement/family learning over the period 1989–2007. These are introduced in the tradition of the reflective practitioner, for whom reflective practice is a continuous process, involving the learner considering critical incidents in her personal or professional experiences (Moon, 1999, pp. 63–5). Reflective practice involves the analysis or evaluation of professional experiences, in a spirit of seeking continuous improvement and greater metacognition (Biggs, 1999, p. 6). A reflective practitioner takes a problem-solving approach to their task (Moon, 1999, p. 63) and will typically have a concern for social justice (Calderhead, 2006). Critics of reflective practice are concerned with its connection to the production of individual knowledge, querying the value of one person's account of a phenomenon which is not shared in the public domain. This criticism, however, ignores not only the dialogical component of reflective practice and the potential for communities of practice to improve learning and develop professional awareness, but also the practice of sharing that learning with the wider professional community (Clouder, 2000) and testing it against other forms of research and theoretical writing.

The reflective passages are linked with research and other writings and with the values of family learning already established.

◀REFLECTION▶━━━━━━━━━━━━━━━━━━━━━━━━━━━━━━━━━━━━━

I first embarked on home school work in 1989 in a housing estate in Port Glasgow, an industrial town in central Scotland whose residents suffered from intergenerational unemployment. My job was to visit parents in their homes and to encourage them to become involved in their children's education. I was overwhelmed by the welcome I received from parents who politely and patiently listened to me talk about how they could support their child's learning. Enthused by the warmth of the response, I worked with the school staff to prepare a comfortable parents' room and devise a programme of parent workshops, volunteering opportunities and drop-in facilities. The teachers worked hard to produce workshops that seemed to go well, and the small number of parents who attended them seemed to find them helpful. However, I was puzzled by the discrepancy between the parents' obvious commitment to their children's learning and the apparent lack of interest in the workshops, volunteering or indeed joining the school board. I talked with the parents in their homes and tried to find out where we were going wrong. Gradually I began to unravel the issues of role expectations and the disparity of power that prevented the development of better home–school relations.

• •

Parental roles

Teachers' expectations of the parental role are complex, their definition problematic and the boundaries that surround them areas for conflict. Carol Vincent identified the four possibilities offered to parents as *supporter/learner, consumer, independent* and *participant* (Vincent, 1993, pp. 43–6), and suggested that the first role as supporter/learner is the one most favoured by professionals, in spite of the prominence of the parent as consumer model under the market-orientated discourse prevalent since the 1980s (Munn 1993, p. 2). Joyce Epstein has been in the forefront of the study of parental involvement in the USA for many years. She created a typology of parental involvement, identifying six categories or types of involvement that she listed as parenting, communicating, volunteering, learning at home, decision-making and collaborating with the community (Epstein 2002, pp. 8–10). These categories have been used extensively by researchers and practitioners to describe and to analyse parental involvement (for example, Juslin and Bremberg, 2008) and are mirrored to some extent in the three types of parental involvement outlined in the Guidance to the Scottish Schools (Parental Involvement) Act (Scottish Executive, 2006a). This typology has helped identify the different means that authorities use to engage with parents and the different effects.

From the perspective of family learning, these descriptions of parental involvement in children's learning, although they offer some insight, also have underlying assumptions that may conflict with the values of family learning. For example the Scottish Executive's three 'levels of engagement' model assumes that 'learning in the home' is the first step in an engagement that proceeds to the higher forms of engagement: that is, partnership with schools and parental representation. Epstein's typology accepts without question the role expectations of the school system, without taking a more critical analysis of how these imposed roles and functions may inhibit how families function in relation to learning and schools. A discussion of the roles that parents play therefore benefits from a more critical analysis.

Parents supporting learning

Although the Scottish Executive asserts that 'Parents are the first and ongoing educators of their own children', it also suggests that 'learning at home' is regarded as dependant on advice and support from the school (Scottish Executive, 2006a, p. 6). Such notions of learning in the home are located within the traditional approaches to learning, rather than within the humanist and social/situational approaches on which family learning is based, as outlined in Chapter 1. These descriptions of learning at home are characterised by an imposition of school curriculum and professional knowledge. They assume that parental involvement must be in *schooling*, rather than *learning*. Maria de Carvalho, in her more recent study of parental involvement in the USA, found similar role confusion between home and school:

> by defining the home as a learning setting for the school curriculum and imposing on the parents a certain educative (parenting) model – education policy is in fact extending political regulation into the diffuse realm of the family and private life, particularly affecting working class and lower middle class families. (De Carvalho, 2001, p. 46)

In some cases, the role of the parent in learning at home has become one where parents are expected to take on the role of quasi teacher. Many parents resist teachers' expectation that they should know detail of how the curriculum is delivered. They believe these are matters for the teacher to manage, and they cannot conceive why they should concern parents. Home and the family are seen as being quite distinct institutions, with different purposes and responsibilities. Like aircraft passengers, many parents are content to buckle their own seatbelts, but are not interested in flying the plane. They prefer to have the relationship with their child's school that they have with their dentist, ensuring dental care is carried out in the home, but having no need to understand the fine detail of the dentist's craft (McBeth, 1993, pp. 28–30).

◤REFLECTION◥ ──────────────────────────────

During the implementation of the Scottish Schools (Parental Involvement) Act in 2007, I had responsibility for organising consultation on a local authority's parental involvement strategy (East Renfrewshire Council, 2007). These events took the form of open space enquiry (Owen, 1997). The groups of parents attending each event defined for themselves the topics they wished to discuss. The main issue raised by all of the groups was the role of parents in homework. Parents reported having to instruct their children in the exercises given, and even for the most well educated parents, this presented dilemmas. Parents who may have studied science at university did not feel at ease instructing their fourth year children in how to do their physics homework. They were anxious that what they taught might not meet current curriculum requirements. They also voiced the view that they could not expect to have current knowledge of all the subjects that the children were being taught. The supervision of homework, something they readily accepted as their role, had become teaching, for which they were not prepared.

These parents, mainly middle class, well educated, articulate and confident, were not rebelling against the dominant culture of the school. They held sufficient stake in the system to be confident of being listened to and being able to influence decision-making. They were conforming to the role that as partners with the schools they were involved in representation and decision-making. This contrasted strongly with an event I held as part of the same consultation with a smaller group of socially excluded parents. Their response was classically ritualistic; they struggled through homework with little hope of being able to help their children, and with the assumption that it was their fault they could not do so. They did not question the homework set, and were resigned to their children not succeeding.

• •

Schools are necessarily highly structured settings. Teachers provide specialised knowledge about cognitive development and academic subjects and prepare children to be tested in these subjects. School teaching is therefore a highly controlled and prescribed task, with educational activities designed and initiated by the teachers. This will remain the case under the *Curriculum for Excellence*, where, in spite of considerable liberation of the school curriculum from tight subject boundaries, there will be clearly defined learning experiences, specified outcomes and an integrated system of assessment (Learning and Teaching Scotland, 2009). As pupils learn in different ways and at different paces, the role of the teacher is highly complex and demanding. The role of the parent as educator is much more fluid, opportunistic, and can be initiated by the child and by social and domestic situations as they arise (Tizard and Hughes, 2002, p. 22). The nearest the learning spheres of home and school come to intersecting is at the pre-school stage, where learning is largely structured around play. It is therefore not surprising that home and school relations are usually healthiest at the pre-school stage. The degree to which school and home learning contribute to learning is impossible to assess, however, a model that derives from the fact that children and young people spend only 15 per cent of their waking hours in school has been devised by McBeth. While there is no statistical basis for the model, it helps to problematise the assumption prevalent in policies that education is the same thing as schooling (McBeth, 1993, pp. 36–7).

Parents as learners

Parents are often regarded as deficient in their knowledge, especially if they are working-class or from a minority ethnic group. They can be regarded as requiring instruction in curriculum matters, basic education, parenting skills and/or skills for the labour market. Parents of children with additional support have reported feelings of anger at the condescension of their child's teachers, in some cases feeling that they are treated as though they also had learning difficulties (Gorman, 2004, p. 19). It is as though the educative enterprise of school becomes so absorbing that everyone becomes a potential pupil. Nowhere is this more insidious than in the traditional 'curriculum workshop'. These sessions rarely involve genuine dialogue and problem-solving between teacher and parent. More often, they consist of instruction from school staff on an area of teacher expertise, followed by questions and answers, or a practical opportunity to try out some of the classroom activities that children experience. Nothing quite matches the experience of fumbling about with unfamiliar classroom materials under the watchful eye of a teacher to make parents feel inadequate and distanced from their child's learning.

Groups of parents may also be seen as a captive audience for adult literacies and adult learning staff seeking to enrol adult learners. As parents of nursery and primary school aged children tend of necessity to congregate at school gates, adult educators will often plan to meet with them there, informally handing out leaflets and talking with parents, or seeking invitations to speak to an organised group activity within the school. Where good working partnerships have developed between schools and community learning and development sections, planned approaches to recruiting adult learners can be productive for both agencies and for the learners involved. However, there can be tensions between the primary focus of family learning on the family as a unit, versus the primary focus of adult education on the adult learner. Such tensions have not been helped by the lack of a specific requirement for community learning and development to provide family learning. Although the Early Years Framework signals a change by identifying parenting and the early years as a priority for community learning and development (Scottish Government, 2008, p. 17), it is not specific in describing what is meant by family learning. For parents for whom adult learning is not a key priority at that point in their lives, the assumption can appear to be an unwelcome intrusion into family life.

Parents as consumers

In the market-oriented political environment that has prevailed in the UK since the 1980s, education is regarded as a commodity rather than a public service, and parents are regarded as consumers. Education is seen as a product paid for by consumers through their taxes. As consumers, parents may influence provision through market forces. Since the Education (Scotland) Act of 1981, parents have had the right to chose their child's school, yet this legislation does not provide an equal choice; parents with less disposable income may be unable to fund the cost of additional travel or meet the greater demands made by schools in more affluent neighbourhoods in terms of school uniform, school trips and after school activities. Since the Act, this quasi-market has contributed to the erosion of the comprehensive ideal of Scottish education and 'sink' and 'magnet' schools have emerged (Mackenzie, 2008, p. 767). Parents may also exercise their consumer role through voicing their views on the quality of the service through structures such as parent councils. The consumer model has persisted into the new millennium, as evidenced by the tone of the Scottish Schools (Parental Involvement) Act 2006, which deals almost exclusively with the representative role in parental involvement to the exclusion of the promotion of learning in the home. Although the Guidance to the Act (Scottish Executive, 2006a, pp. 6–7) makes passing reference to learning in the home, the bulk of the document is devoted to issues of representation. Despite the evidence that parental representation is the form of parental involvement in learning that has least impact on learning and attainment, the Scottish Executive still pursued a consumer model, and the sweeping changes that were expected did not materialise. School Boards were replaced by Parent Councils, which although less formal and bureaucratic in their nature, are similar to their predecessors and are likely to evidence as little parental involvement in learning or desire to become involved with schools as the Boards (Aitken, 2008, p. 157). This mirrors the earlier English experience, where increasing the role of the parent as consumer has not led to any identifiable improvement in home–school relations (Vincent, 1996, p. 35).

Parents as volunteers

This view of parents is heavily gendered, based on the notion that mothers have free time during the day while their child is at school to support school activities. Recruited groups of parents, sometimes called 'Mums' armies' are used to make up deficits in the school provision, escorting children on trips, tidying and sorting equipment, preparing materials and other tasks which are seen as detracting from the teacher's time to teach. The rhetoric suggests benefits to parents in terms of their own understanding of their children's learning, however, it is rare to find parent volunteers engaged in actual learning activities with the children. Nonetheless, many parents experience volunteering in their child's school as an activity that raises confidence to take up further learning opportunities and community activities, and for some it provides the first rung of a ladder that may lead them back into employment. In its best forms, volunteering can promote social capital and build local capacity (McGivney, 2000, p. 47). Sadly, parent volunteers are all too often roped in to make up the number of adults required for a school outing, or to supervise a school disco. Perhaps the most negative aspect of parent volunteering is the lack of transparency about its objectives. The recruitment of volunteers is often cloaked in the rhetoric of partnership with parents, with assumed concomitant benefits for learning, whereas it is much more often driven by a need for more human resource. It is rare to find schools with developed policies and strategies for recruiting, training and supporting volunteers, or celebrating their contribution. Local authorities could perform a useful function in developing such policies and providing central services to support schools that choose to recruit volunteers.

Parents as scapegoats

Blaming or indeed praising parents for how their children turn out is so deeply ingrained in our culture that we find it hard to think differently about the role of parenting in children's development (Alexander, 1996, p. 15). We tend to privatise our view of things, and to ignore the influence of wider society. Parents often fulfil the very useful role of scapegoat for their children's failure to conform to expected modes of behaviour in the school setting. Yet behaviour is always context-specific. Children rarely behave in school the way they do at home; the culture and expectations are quite different. The notion that children are influenced in behaviour by their parents has recently been challenged by Judith Rich Harris, who found that children are more likely to be influenced in their behaviour by their peers than by their parents (Harris, 1998, p. 2). In her ground-breaking study of the influences on child development, Harris challenges the belief that parents are the most important factor in child development. Harris rejects the time-honoured 'nature versus nurture' debate, on the grounds that 'nurture' implies rearing, a task we normally associate with parents. She replaces 'nurture' with 'environment' and dismisses many of our treasured notions about the extent to which parents influence their children, placing much more emphasis on the peer group. The notion that repugnant behaviours we observe in children might not be as much the parents' fault as we had thought is an uncomfortable one for those for whom the staff room mantra has been, 'I blame the parents.' It is always uncomfortable to find our model for understanding some aspect of our lives no longer fits. Yet our model needs to develop, if only because blaming the parents and seeking to educate them has not been effective in improving educational outcomes.

Parents as partners

The most dominant expectation of parents in public discourse on education is that they be partners in their child's education. However, there is wide variation in the types of partnership that parents are invited to join. Partnership is a wonderful example of a good word that sometimes keeps bad company. The word implies cooperation and responsibility for the achievement of a specified goal in a shared enterprise, however, the rhetoric is not always born out in reality.

In its most enlightened form, parental partnership allows parents to play a full and equal role in their child's education. Though the formal curriculum remains the business of the school, the role of parents in helping their children in a wide range of informal ways is acknowledged, supported and celebrated.

◀ REFLECTION ▬▬▬▬▬▬▬▬▬▬▬▬▬▬▬▬▬▬▬▬▬▬▬▬

I enjoyed a true partnership with my son's primary school. I had adopted a 10-year-old boy whose education had been seriously disrupted – before I adopted him he had never attended a mainstream school, and he could barely read. His teachers were enormously committed to providing formal classroom learning suitable for his needs, welcoming my co-operation and suggestions, while encouraging me to help him learn at home and in his community. I recognised their expertise in planning and delivering a specialised curriculum, and they recognised my expertise at providing stimulus, enrichment and skills through involving him in a range of very ordinary family and community experiences. Both of his teachers accepted my advice that formal homework was counterproductive and recognised my son would learn more effectively doing different things with his out-of-school time. Progress during the 18 months he spent at primary school was dramatic, and he entered secondary school able to keep up with his peers.

• •

Parents are often seen as token partners, invited to support learning only in ways determined by the school, for example through ensuring the completion of homework and receiving information on academic progress. The persistence of the one-way nature of much communication between home and school can be illustrated through personal learning planning, introduced in Scotland through the new community school's initiative (Scottish Office, 1998). It was then envisaged as a three-way dialogue between parent, child and teacher. This official view remains in force. Personal learning planning is described as 'a conversation about learning that will involve you, your child and their teacher' (Scottish Executive, 2006c, p. 4), however, the reality is that most personal learning planning takes place between the child and the teacher, with parents being asked simply to review and sign the plan. One of the main reasons for not having a three-way conversation given is time; with around 10 minutes twice a year available for a teacher to meet with a child's parent, it is difficult to imagine a constructive dialogue taking place. The allocation of time to meeting with parents is in itself an indicator of how parental partnership is given a very low priority. The 2001 national agreement with the teacher unions, popularly known as the McCrone Settlement, stated that extra time be allocated to partnership with parents, but this activity was only one in a long list of other activities. The detail of the time allocation was left to schools to negotiate (Scottish Executive, 2006a, p. 6). Behind the government's rhetoric of parental partnership there is little in the way of incentive or directive.

How parents respond to the notion of partnership is instructive. Parents that experience social exclusion because of living in poverty, with disability or being of a minority ethnic group sometimes show a ritualistic response to the expectations that they will be partners. They go through the motions, attending meetings, signing the report cards and the personal learning plans. They abide by the restrictions placed on parents' access to the school but having very little real sense of being involved in a partnership. Others will simply give up the struggle and opt out, forming the group of parents who are often viewed as 'apathetic' by school staff.

Disparity of power

Concern that parents may have too much power in the running of schools has been expressed by professionals. The consumer model of parental involvement already mentioned has indeed offered parents political power which has been used to influence government policy (Munn, 1993, pp. 91–4; Gillespie, 2008, pp. 195–6), but the evidence of parents influencing decision making at the local level of the school is less evident. There seems to be little appetite among parents in Scotland to take control of schools. Parents have shown little interest overall in the provision for schools opting out of local authority control as introduced in the School Boards (Scotland) Act, or in the governance arrangement of the school boards and parent councils (Aitken, 2008, pp. 154, 157). Moreover, there is evidence that when parents have tried to use the School Board to influence change, the School Board itself can act to protect the status quo (Munn, 1993, p. 92). These analyses of power relations between home and school consider outward, manifest power and tend to involve a small number of articulate and politically engaged parents. The issues of power between home and school from the perspective of family learning are more subtle.

The imbalance of power between home and school is perhaps best understood not as a simple imposition of authority from the school, but as a subtle compact between home and school, where the school is dominant in the child's education and the parent tacitly agrees to be subordinate, albeit while occasionally outwardly resisting. An example of this is provided in Chapter 3, This notion of active consent was proposed by Antonio Gramsci and termed cultural hegemony. Gramsci regarded it as operating through the institutions of society, such as the press, the church and the school, which function to make particular values, beliefs and attitudes become accepted (Vincent, 1996, pp. 3–6; Vincent and Warren, 1998, p. 178). One of the ways this operates is through the tacit acceptance of what constitutes worthwhile knowledge and learning.

◀REFLECTION▶─────────────────────

Some of the families I worked with were settled travelling people, with an extensive knowledge of natural history, who passed this knowledge on to their children. Others were unemployed welders and craftsmen from the obsolete shipyards, with creative and practical talents to share. Almost all of them had strong links through extended families and neighbourhood networks that provided children with diverse and supportive learning opportunities. The council flats occupied by many of these families had long, narrow corridors, with high ceilings. One particular group of families I grew to know used these corridors for storing small boats or canoes, suspended expertly by a system of pulleys. The boats were hand made from found materials, and were used in summer to take the families across the Clyde estuary, up the short River Leven and into Loch Lomond, where the families would camp on a small island for most of the summer. The children in these camps were not only having a cheap summer holiday, they were also learning all sorts of social and practical skills. Nonetheless, most of the school staff regarded the families in that neighbourhood as at best inadequate, and at worst dysfunctional. They valued their own specialised knowledge of the curriculum and child development over the parents' cultural knowledge and understanding of how their children learned. The language of power was critical to this disconnection; parents struggled to express what they did with their children in the elaborated code familiar to school staff.

• •

Under the hegemony of the school, school practices and school knowledge are given a greater validity than home routines and home learning. Some parents view the school as operating subtle penalties for parents who do not conform, and fear that if they did not comply their children may be less fairly treated at school. These are not only social class power struggles; they are also issues of gender. Mothers spoke to me of the expectations of their role both at home and at school – as home–school partnership activities take place largely during the working day, there is an expectation that women attend, and the feminisation of activities tends to debar fathers who might otherwise have been involved. Moreover, there can be a marked difference between the information about school held by those mothers who are more involved with day-to-day practices in the school. Kathy Maclachlan conducted a study of parental involvement and the mothering role in Glasgow that revealed not only that working mothers, although heavily involved in their children's learning, were not recognised as doing so due to their non-involvement in schools. Between the best intentions of the parents and head teachers in the research group, there were areas of tension and conflict in which the working mothers were less powerful to voice their agenda and control the outcome (Maclachlan, 1996, pp. 31–6).

Consensus and discord

Across the UK, there is a general consensus that good relations between home and school are beneficial for a child's learning and strong evidence to suggest that most parents wish to be actively involved in their children's learning

(Dyson and Robson, 2002). In Scotland, the duty to promote good relations is laid down in legislation, most recently in the Scottish Schools (Parental Involvement) Act (Scottish Executive, 2006b). The quality of parent school partnerships is a topic for self-evaluation and is also subject to inspection (HMIe, 2007a, p. 33). Most school websites and school handbooks speak positively about the school's commitment to home school relations. In spite of such apparent public consent, much effort to promote parental participation remains superficial, perfunctory and ineffective (Vincent, 1996, p. 73). The difficulties in reforming parental participation are not unique to the Scottish or UK setting – similar difficulties have been identified in the USA (Anderson, 1998, p. 573) and in the Republic of Ireland (Hanafin and Lynch, 2002, p. 38), where participation was found to be a way to create institutional legitimacy for current educational practices, rather than a means of extending democracy. Coleman, in his extensive research into the effectiveness of home–school relations in British Columbia, outlines and dismisses as myth four views that teachers commonly hold. Although Coleman was writing about the Canadian public school system, these myths are ones that in my experience still prevail in many Scottish staff rooms:

Myth 1   *Some parents don't care about school and schooling;*
Myth 2   *Some parents cannot help their children to be successful in school;*
Myth 3   *Parents are involved and influential in school at present;*
Myth 4   *Parent involvement is a way for parents to control schools.*

(Coleman, 1998, pp. 143–8)

These myths are developed and sustained because of a basic misunderstanding about human behaviour, described as the Fundamental Attribution Error, which is a tendency to interpret other people's behaviour by overestimating the importance of their personality and underestimating the situation and the context (Storms, 1997, p. 175). We tend to place too much importance on what we believe to be the failings of parents and too little on the systems and structures through which they must negotiate their entry into the partnership we seek to promote. Thus, parents who are taciturn in formal teacher–parent meetings may become keenly involved in dialogue about their child's learning in a more relaxed context.

Summary

The study of role expectations for parents exposes issues of power and conformity. It also reveals and helps us understand the behaviours of professionals and parents more clearly. Many social psychologists believe that much of human behaviour comes about because of living up to the expectations of others or playing the role that others expect us to play. We do not all choose to conform neatly to these roles, however. The extent to which we are likely to conform is understood to be dependent on the extent to which we feel we hold a stake in the culture, and believe we are likely to achieve the ends that the culture values. The classic responses of individuals who do not conform to role expectation have been described as innovation, ritualism, retreat or rebellion (Fulcher and Scott, 1999, p. 48). Applying this in the context of the culture of schooling (with its specified ends of academic attainment and enhanced life chances) it is conceivable that parents who feel they are likely to be able to achieve these ends for their children will conform, while those who do not may choose other stances. They may innovate by bending the rules: for example, a parent may do her child's homework and pretend it is the child's own work in order to achieve some peace within the household. They may approach parental involvement in a ritualistic fashion, going through the motions with little commitment: for example, attending a parents' meeting with little commitment to the notion of parent/teacher dialogue. They may retreat by dropping out of contact with school. They may rebel and challenge the conventional value of the schools, although the act of rebellion does depend on having some confidence that the culture can be changed. This application of role theory suggests we pay close attention to the role expectations that schools place on parents, so we can better understand some of the responses.

Despite the evidence from research and observation of current practice that relationships between home and school can be affected negatively by role confusion, power imbalances and subtle forms of self-control, across Scotland there are many successful attempts to create different outcomes using family learning approaches. Some of these practices are described in Chapter 3.

Family learning practice across Scotland

It wasn't like a classroom, more like real life . . . we talked about it for ages afterwards. *(Parent, Glenlee Primary School, South Lanarkshire)*

Surprisingly little is known about the practice of family learning across Scotland. This chapter describes firstly what is known from an official perspective and secondly what has been obtained from a study of practice I carried out in 2008 while researching for this book. The study included a survey of practice in all Scottish local authorities, telephone interviews with key informants and field visits. The study has resulted in case studies that are based on emergent themes, including working with excluded groups, and school- and community-based practice. There is no attempt to quantify practice, but rather to consider how these emergent themes help us to understand the nature of family learning in Scotland. The case studies make it apparent that there is a great deal of activity and enthusiasm for family learning across Scotland. However, government reports have only recently begun to compile this information.

For local government purposes, Scotland is divided into 32 council areas governed by unitary authorities responsible for all local government functions, including schools, adult learning and community development. The councils have considerable autonomy for how services are managed under the Scottish Government, an autonomy that has increased since a concordat was agreed between the Government and the Councils (Scottish Government, 2007a). Since 2004, Community Health Partnerships (CHPs) have been established across Scotland as part of the modernisation of the National Health Service. CHPs are charged with establishing substantive partnership with local authorities, and to act as a focus for integrating health services and delivering on health improvement. There therefore exists a diverse range of departmental, corporate and partnership arrangements for the delivery of services that are likely to be most involved in family learning: that is, the schools section, libraries and information services, community learning and development and health. Agencies not under the management of local authorities, such as health services, further education and the voluntary sector, also have a role in providing family learning. The range of possible models has distinct advantages. It allows for creative approaches, and a mix of partnerships arrangements designed to meet local needs using local capacity. It encourages grassroots movements and local networking among the professionals involved. However, it also leads to patchy provision across the country. As family learning is not a statutory requirement it can be overlooked, especially in the lean years, as local authorities allocate funding to other aspects of work which are required by government.

Only a limited perspective on the extent of family learning across Scotland can be obtained through the inspection process, as there is no distinct focus on family learning in inspections. The education functions of local authorities were inspected by HMIe between 2001 and 2005, and a second round of inspections was in progress by 2008. These inspections include all education functions, and therefore include adult learning and some community learning and development tasks. In five of these inspections, HMIe commented on family learning. One good practice example of family learning's impact on fathers was identified in Aberdeen City.

The community learning and development functions of local authorities are also inspected by HMIe. Community learning and development has three national priorities: achievement through learning for adults, achievement through learning for young people and achievement through building community capacity. It is also seen as contributing to personal development (Scottish Executive, 2004a, p. 1). HMIe includes family learning as an example of a possible community learning and development activity.

Community learning and development inspections focus on communities within local authorities. Of the 72 published reports, 32 mentioned family learning, usually by including it in a list of other activities, although there were also a small number of family learning activities described in more detail as good practice examples. Family learning may be included in reports under the heading of personal development:

Inspections of personal development with adults evaluate learning groups in the community such as formal classes, family learning groups, literacy and numeracy groups and individual tuition, and aspects of adult guidance. Typically HM Inspectors visit and observe groups, classes and individual tuition. They interview staff and adult learners. The principal focus is on the extent to which learners are achieving positive outcomes in relation to their individual, family and working life and to their development as active citizens. (HMIe, 2004, p. 2)

Councils will normally have the opportunity to signpost inspectors towards discrete aspects of community learning and development in their area. One published report described how an inspection in East Renfrewshire in 2004 examined family learning in detail as a discrete area of work that was found to be 'very good' overall – this was before the HMIe introduced the category of 'excellent'. The family learning service was found to be very good at engaging and supporting excluded individuals, providing learning activities in multi-agency contexts, planning and delivering family learning and providing very good learning experiences for the family participants (HMIe, 2004, pp. 8–10).

In 2007–8, HMIE began to trawl inspection reports looking for evidence of family learning and the impact that family learning programmes may have on attainment and wider achievement in the early years, based on outcomes for adults, children, schools and the wider community. This evidence was used to inform the Early Years Framework (Scottish Government, 2008). It found that programmes of family learning are reported upon within inspection reports on other services but these findings are subsumed within wider evaluative sections and there is a lack of a discrete focus within the reports. As a result, HMIe planned to develop a larger investigation during 2008–9 into the impacts of family learning. This task will consider for the first time the impact of family learning in all services inspected by HMIe (HMIe, 2008), signalling the increased attention that HMIe is paying to the value of family learning.

While HMIe is responsible for ensuring public accountability and improving standards in education, Learning and Teaching Scotland (LTS) is a public body charged with providing guidance on the implementation of government policy in schools and pre-5 settings. It is an executive non-departmental public body sponsored by the Scottish Government and is the lead organisation for curriculum development in Scotland. It has responsibility for promoting parents as partners in learning, and for providing advice on the implementation of the Scottish Schools (Parental Involvement) Act (2006). It has appointed a

National Parental Involvement Co-ordinator and together with Parental Involvement Field Officers, it highlights examples of good practice in parental involvement on its website. These include some examples of family learning.

The only recent study of family learning in Scotland has been conducted from within the community learning and development sector. A report by the Linked Work and Training Trust (LWTT) examined the definitions used, the contexts where family learning appears, and the impact on raising aspirations and widening access to further and higher education. The report concluded that there is little evidence of what makes some programmes in family learning more successful than others, nor is there a clear view of what constitutes 'success'. The report contains some case studies and analyses of different models in family learning (Jones and Macrae, 2008).

In 2008, I conducted a study on the extent of family learning across Scotland, which included sending a questionnaire to the chief executives of the 32 councils. I received 18 responses from a range of officers including managers of community learning and development, a manager of community regeneration, a manager of integrated community schools and one head of education services. One response came from a family learning manager. There were also responses from a family learning worker, a home link teacher and a social worker. Of the 18 councils that responded, 14 reported having a family learning service in their council area, although not all of these used the term 'family learning'. The strategic management of family learning in these 14 councils was varied. The Scottish Schools (Parental Involvement) Act of 2006 placed a new duty on councils to draw up a parental involvement strategy. In only five of the councils responding to the survey was family learning mentioned or included in the council's parental involvement strategy. Several councils reported that family learning took place across a range of different council departments, but that there was no clear strategic lead. Eleven councils had arrangements for assuring the quality of family learning, and all of these reported using *How Good is Our Community Learning and Development?* (HMIE, 2006c) or the Learning Evaluation and Planning (LEAP) tool (Scottish Government, 2007b). Ten of the responses were followed up by telephone interviews and three field visits were made to build materials for the case study later in this chapter.

On consideration of the evidence presented both from the publications of the public and voluntary sectors and my own study, some key themes emerged. These are explored below, using examples of practice from across Scotland. The examples used are by no means exhaustive, nor do they necessarily imply the best practice. They serve only to illustrate the emergent themes.

Developments within schooling

From the evidence presented by public bodies, it is clear that family learning, unlike parental involvement, is not generally regarded as a central function of schooling, although many schools are involved in family learning and have externally recognised good practice. The absence of family learning from the parental involvement strategies in many of the councils is informative. It seems that in considering parental involvement in schools sections, some education services have not yet made the link with what their colleagues in other agencies are achieving in family learning. While local support for family learning among families and practitioners across Scotland is staunch, there is in many cases a lack of a strategic lead and commitment. Moreover, support for family learning can be a victim of departmentalism. As long as it is not a required function within a department, there is a tendency to consider it the function of some other group.

Strategic approaches

As long as there is no legislative requirement to promote family learning and no comprehensive inspection process to provide public accountability, family learning thrives only where there is local commitment, often as the result of key personnel who have had the vision to spearhead the approach. This leadership may be at the strategic level within the council area, or at a more local level, within a community or school. Strategic approaches within councils offer opportunities for joined-up approaches through shared responsibility for policy development, planning, delivery and quality assurance. Services can be delivered efficiently, and where roles are clearly defined, there is the possibility of all relevant sections and external agencies playing their part. Two examples of strategic approaches were found, one in South Lanarkshire and one in East Renfrewshire.

South Lanarkshire Council serves some of the most deprived communities in Scotland, and has the fifth largest population of people living in the most deprived communities (Scottish Government, 2007c). The Council has had a strategic commitment to partnership with parents since 1991, and provided resources to maintain a well-established Home School Partnership team that has a strong focus on family learning in addition to promoting parental involvement in schools. Having been established for many years, the Home School Partnership has had time to develop strong relationships and credibility in the communities and in the schools. Although the team's programme has developed over the years since the partnership started, the guiding principle has been constant: 'Engaging mums, dads and adult carers in their children's learning raises attainment and achievement and produces better outcomes for families' (South Lanarkshire Council, 2007, p. 3). Although a dedicated partnership team leads the initiative, the strength of the model is derived from the extent to which practice is embedded in school practice across the Council area and in association with other agencies, including health. A wide range of resources is used, most of which has been designed within South Lanarkshire. Each resource has a teacher's pack and an associated in-service opportunity, normally lead by a teacher who has successfully used the resource. The staff development model has resulted in a growing commitment among school staff to the notion that family activities can have a strong influence on learning. Each of the resources is linked clearly to the dimensions of *A Curriculum for Excellence* (Scottish Executive, 2004a), and this has been of particular support to teachers as they develop programmes for the new curriculum. The Home School Partnership website (www.hsp.lanlinks.org) provides easy public access to information and tips to support learning in the home, along with information on the extensive range of programmes and activities offered. The impact of the Home School Partnership has consistently been rated highly by HMIe inspections in South Lanarkshire, in the schools inspections, the inspections of the education functions and in the inspections of community learning and development.

A range of new initiatives were launched by the Scottish Office and the Scottish Executive between 1997 and 2005 under a variety of funding streams such as the Excellence Fund, the National Priorities Action Fund and the New Opportunities Fund. These funding streams resulted in programmes in early literacy, new community schools, family literacy and behaviour support, but they posed challenges for councils in the management, accounting and mainlining of short-term projects. At the end of the first phase of funding of New Community Schools in 2002, East Renfrewshire Council chose to amalgamate several projects working with families under one theme, resulting in the establishment of a dedicated Family Learning Service. Although the Family Learning Service was established within the section of the education services responsible for schools, it has taken from its inception a community learning and development approach to working with families. The service is unique in being the only one inspected by HMIe as a discrete entity when it was included in a community learning and development inspection in 2004. That inspection found that the service had 'very good' practice in engagement and support, learning opportunities, delivery and learning experience – the highest level awarded by HMIe at that time:

> The learning experience of the participants in family learning was very good. The learners were able to describe their growth in self-esteem, confidence in their committee skills and in running a programme of activities. Most facilities provided a very good environment for learning. Staff created a motivating and stimulating atmosphere and had very good relationships with participants. Staff negotiated clear outcomes with learners. Learners took responsibility for their learning with the family learning coordinators. The worker at Busby Primary School played a supportive role with parents organising a summer activity programme. Staff ensured that there was a good variety of challenge and creativity offered to participants.
>
> For example, parents were involved in the organisation of the *Summer Heatwave* programme funded through the New Opportunities Fund. Learners were aware of their learning and the impact it was having on their personal development. (HMIe 2004)

HMIe further reported on a range of positive impacts of the service in an inspection of the education functions of East Renfrewshire in 2007. These positive impacts included the development of parents' confidence, more parental involvement in children's learning, and progression to other adult learning opportunities. East Renfrewshire has one of the most diverse populations in Scotland. The appointment of specialist staff to promote better access for minority ethnic families has been a key strength of the service. Family Learning is a strong element with the Council's parental involvement strategy and the principles of the Family Learning Strategy have been adopted for the new Parental Involvement Strategy (East Renfrewshire Council, 2007). These principles were drawn from guidance for community learning and development (Scottish Executive 2004b).

Grassroots movements

In contrast to strategic developments, some areas are more dependent on growth from the grassroots of the organisation, where a collegiate approach arises as workers see the need for more co-ordinated approaches. Such grassroots development has often taken place where local circumstances pose unique challenges. The Shetland Islands has the second smallest population of a council area in Scotland, spread out across a vast archipelago comprising 16 inhabited islands. Providing specialist services across such a sparse population poses peculiar challenges, although the small rural communities also enjoy the advantage of the school being the centre of community living and learning. Shetland has a sole home link teacher who promotes parental involvement and family learning throughout Shetland and who has been instrumental in establishing a local network of workers from a range of agencies who have a role in family learning, including active schools, community learning and development, health and libraries. The network has enhanced the delivery of family learning activities across the area, through the sharing of expertise and resources. The very scarcity of professionals dedicated to family learning is potentially beneficial: schools are provided with resources, advice and support, but have to take most of the responsibility for the delivery of family learning themselves, potentially leading to a more embedded and sustainable service.

Established in 2001, the Scottish Network for Parental Involvement in Learning (SNPICL) is a voluntary organisation, which has grown out of a grassroots movement among a broad range of professionals looking for mutual support and the sharing of good practice. It has both a national and a local focus, with five local networks supporting practitioners across Scotland, using video conferencing to reach colleagues in remote areas. The annual conference provides a national opportunity to share good practice and to promote the approach with others, including politicians and national bodies. Since the Scottish Schools (Parental Involvement Act (2006), interest in the Network has grown and the annual conference is highly popular. A research report on the role of SNPICL made recommendations for the voluntary organisation, including: the promotion of the professional identity of those working in the field; researching the training needs of its members; enhancing the national profile; developing quality indicators that would demonstrate the value of the work, and seeking funding to implement these recommendations (McArdle, 2007, p. 37).

Working with excluded groups

Families from excluded groups may face particular challenges in engaging with schools, which often tend to reflect and cater for the mainstream dominant culture. Examples of excluded groups include people with chronic illness or disability, some minority ethnic communities, prisoners and those living in poverty. It can also include male parents, and parents of children who experience behavioural difficulties while at school.

It is common for schools to talk about the difficulty of involving certain parents, and to express frustration that they cannot reach the parents they believe need most support to be involved in their children's learning. When parents are aware that their child is presenting behavioural difficulties within the school setting, they can be understandably reluctant to engage, as they may fear shame and embarrassment. They may also be in conflict with the school as a result of disciplinary action against their child.

Nurture groups have been operating in schools since the 1970s, based on theories of attachment (Bowlby, 1969, p. 242). There has been an increase in nurture groups across Scotland in recent years, and the City of Glasgow has made a significant investment in the approach by fully funding 58 nurture groups across the city (City of Glasgow, 2007). The parents of children referred to nurture groups are likely to be among the most disengaged parents. Children referred may display the kinds of behaviour which are associated with a lack of attachment: for example, immaturity, unpredictability, temper tantrums, phobias, aggression and withdrawal (Bishop, 2008, p. 2). In promoting the approach, the Nurture Group Network defines a nurture group as a small supportive class of up to 12 children that provides a secure, predictable environment dedicated to providing for the different developmental needs of each pupil. The Network advises that nurture groups should be staffed by two adults and that pupils should attend regularly for a substantial part of each week (Nurture Group Network, 2008). Although the Network provides information for parents, there is no suggestion that parents can be involved in their child's nurture group. This is not surprising, given that the theories lying behind nurture groups suggest that there has been in some way a failure of parenting, and that the child needs to be 're-parented' (Bishop, 2008, p. 5). In Perth and Kinross, however, parents are actively encouraged to join in some afternoon activities with their children in the nurture groups and many have done so. The activities are designed to engage both children and parents working together in a secure and supportive environment. This has led to greater understanding among all concerned about the difficulties the children experience. Families have been able to make progress in the nurture they can offer to their child as their confidence grows and good parenting practice is modelled by staff. Community link workers, who are responsible for family learning, are able to support the school-based groups by working directly with the adults in the groups. By taking a no-blame approach and working in partnership with other agencies, the schools have been able to engage effectively with some of the most vulnerable children and their parents.

Dads and other male family members can also be hard to reach, given the predominantly female nature of childcare. Several projects in Scotland have had considerable success in engaging effectively with men. The Men and Children Matter programme in Perth and Kinross has successfully involved almost 100 men, including uncles and granddads who have signed up for activities designed to be attractive to men who have responsibility for children. These activities include work with digital cameras, making bird boxes, cycling, fishing and reading with their child. The Family Learning Team in Aberdeen City successfully involved fathers in actively supporting their children's learning through the 'Challenge Dads' programme, supported by literacies funding. Activities included parenting classes, literacy development and a range of self-development activities. HMIe identified the programme as an example of good practice, and found that the programme was successful in developing the self-confidence of parents involved, in enriching their relationships with their children, and in supporting their progression to further education, training and employment (HMIe, 2006b).

Each year, an estimated 13,500 children lose a parent to imprisonment in Scotland, (Loukes, 2004, p. 5). The effects of this loss may be severe, and may include experiences of bereavement, shame, bullying, social exclusion and disruption to learning (Loukes, 2004, p. 7). A number of innovative programmes addressing parenting have been introduced in recent years, including a course run by One Stop Childcare in Her Majesty's Prison (HMP) Edinburgh and the 'Incredible Years' parenting course offered by Highland Addictions Service in HMP Inverness (Loukes, 2006, p. 22). There are currently no examples of promoting family learning in prison in Scotland. In Northern Ireland, however, the child-centred visits scheme is breaking new ground by involving prisoners and their families learning together through the Big Book Share project sponsored by the Paul Hamlyn Foundation. Children's librarians help prisoners choose a book for their child. The prisoner then records himself reading the book, and gives his child the recording (The Reading Agency, 2008). This example of family learning belies the notion that parents have to be seen in schools to be actively supporting their child's learning. There is a need now to equip better schools and other agencies to respond appropriately to the family learning needs of the children of prisoners. A report by Scotland's Commissioner for Children and Young People has described these children as the 'invisible victims of crime and of our penal system. Their voices are silenced by the shame and stigma associated with imprisonment' (SCCYP, 2008, p. 3).

For some parents whose first language is not English there may be special difficulties in communicating with school, and in understanding and being able to communicate with their children about their experiences outside the home. These difficulties can be compounded by the failure of some schools to appreciate the cultural diversity of the communities they serve. The appointment of bilingual family learning workers to reach out to excluded community groups has been a powerful means of breaking down the barriers and helping schools to engage more effectively with families. The range of tasks undertaken by bilingual family learning workers in East Renfrewshire include the development of dual language resources, group work with parents, supporting learning in the home and designing and delivering family learning activities that, while not excluding the dominant culture, are particularly sensitive to cultural diversity.

Physical disabilities can be barriers to families learning together. Over 90 per cent of deaf parents have hearing children and face particular concerns about their involvement in their children's learning. Research into these concerns revealed that many of these surround schooling: for example, not having sufficient access to information about their child's learning and lacking guidance on how to tackle bullying – a special concern for hearing children who may be teased because their parents are deaf (Allsop and Kyle, 1997, p. 9). These parents may not only be isolated from information, but from networks of parents who can support them – and to whom they can also be of support. Excluding such families from family learning by failing to make provision for them is not only detrimental to the deaf; it also potentially denies access for hearing families to all that deaf people can bring to the network. Thornliebank Primary in East Renfrewshire opened up access to a profoundly deaf parent by ensuring an interpreter was present for events the parent wished to attend, resulting in benefits for all those involved (Kandirikirira, 2006, p. 9).

Parents experiencing mental health issues may also face barriers to family learning. A high proportion of adults with mental health issues are also parents, and the incidence of depression is highest among mothers, lone parents and those not in employment. In recognition of the hurdles families with mental health issues have to overcome, the National Institute of Adult Continuing Education (NIACE) launched a new resource for family learning and mental health practitioners called 'Making the Connection' (NIACE, 2008). The stigma associated with mental illness means that it can be difficult for a parent to disclose their health status, and their behaviour may therefore be misunderstood. For example, depression may be seen as apathy and bipolar disorder may be seen as aggression. Schools can play an important part in building the local networks and community well being that can be of support to all parents, especially those who may be isolated or depressed. A family learning programme in East Renfrewshire, described in more detail in Chapter 5, was specifically designed to build community well being through developing parent networking.

The power of the arts

A key theme emerging from the questionnaires, interviews and field visits is the power of the arts to provide contexts in which people, adults and children, can experience personal and social transformation. Many family learning activities bring families together to prepare a dramatic production, compile materials for literacy work, dance, make music or create something visual. While arts activities have positive benefits in providing fun, promoting inclusion and building self-esteem, they do much more than that by developing a sense of connectedness between people, and between people and their environment. The arts, well delivered, can be a powerful contributor to social capital, as described in more detail in Chapter 4. In the school context, the creation of a family production for use in the school can be a positive way for families to contribute to the school, rather than simply be passive recipients of services:

> The arts allow us individually and collectively to connect to the self and yet also distance us from ourselves, acting as a mirror encouraging reflection. They enable people to capture the ineffable; the hard-to-put-into-words allowing them to explore issues which are hard to grasp through number and language alone, for example how it feels to arrive in Scotland as an asylum seeker ... They are more accessible to a wider range of people than many other forms of discourse. The arts can make things visible and memorable since they demand our sensorial, emotional and intellectual attention. They therefore increase the likelihood of people not only finding voice but being heard. (Kandirikirira, 2006, p. 9)

Developing new resources

In addition to a wide range of commercially available resources and the government sponsored programmes such as Bookstart that are commonly used across Scotland, workers in family learning have developed programmes locally that are sometimes breathtaking in their simplicity. Families Reading Together in East Renfrewshire is one such programme, intended for use at the pre-schools stage through to the second year in primary school. Designed to promote literacy, the programme is a combination of storytelling and book lending, however, the crucial aspect is the use of a home–school diary, which encourages parents to read at home with their child and to make comment on the story. Staff respond, maintaining a close dialogue with parents during the time the programme is running, although in some cases they may rarely meet the parent face to face. Parents become rapidly engaged as their child's excitement about reading is kindled by the story telling and kept alive through choosing a book to take home. Crucial to the success of the programme is the dialogue built up through the home school diary, particularly when the staff comments are lively, interesting and prompt further discussion. Evidence from the unpublished pilot scheme evaluation revealed that the initiative appealed to both mums and dads, to grandparents and other adults and also to older siblings. Parents who took part reported reading and talking more with their child. They also reported taking their child to the public library more often or for the first time.

Developing resources with parents can be about more than the product. The process of producing materials for families to use can be a powerful means of increasing learning, confidence, and a wide variety of skills. Responding to the national survey I carried out in 2008, the Family Learning Service in Edinburgh expressed the process as follows:

> Although we produce a lot of things, we feel that the main focus of our groups is on the process, not the product. For example, a story sack project created by a group of parents provides the school with a valuable resource, but for the parents in involved it has meant:
>
> - visiting a bookshop;
> - deciding which books to have;
> - labelling and numbering books;
> - writing supplementary activities for each book;
> - learning computing skills;
> - organising a system for lending;
> - negotiating a system for lending with the school; and
> - organising a rota.

In the course of achieving the outcome, the dialogue between the family learning worker and the parent is continuing and further opportunities to learn are identified in an informal way.

Glenlee Primary, South Lanarkshire: A case study on a school-based approach

In October 2008, I carried out a field visit to a primary school to examine how one school has embedded family learning in its practice. Family learning begins early in the morning at Glenlee Primary. The Breakfast Club in this South Lanarkshire school is staffed by parents who were originally volunteers but are now paid to provide childcare for working parents. Family Learning also starts early in the child's life. Class teachers and other staff visit the homes of new entrants to the nursery to meet with each family in their own comfort zone. The programme for the visits centres on reading a story to the child, an activity which provides an opportunity for some informal assessment, a means of getting to know the child and the parent, and a way of affirming the value of learning in the home. It is important to the school that the good relationships developed with nursery parents are not lost on the child's entry to school and this has led to the introduction of a 'soft start and finish' to the school day for Primary 1 pupils. Linked with an active approach to learning which retains some aspects of the Nursery learning environment in Primary 1, the 'soft start and finish' allows time for parents to witness their child settling into the day and taking responsibility for their learning. Both parents and teachers find the less formal beginning and end to the day aids partnership between home and school. The active learning is so managed in the Primary 1 classrooms during the soft start that children take responsibility for their own learning and teachers are free to speak with parents if necessary.

Glenlee Primary has recently moved into a new school building, and family learning has been built into the fabric through the provision of parent rooms in both the nursery and the school. This provides a useful context for the services of a Home School Partnership Worker for two days a week. The parents value having a professional member of staff that they described as 'not hiding behind a professional barrier', while appreciating her knowledge and understanding of educational issues affecting their children. While they reported that teaching staff were friendly and approachable, they acknowledged that they tended to set teachers 'on a pedestal', according them deferential treatment on account of their training and experience, and being awed by their ability to manage the curriculum for a class of children. By contrast, the home–school worker was seen to be encouraging parents to see their own potential, both as learners themselves, but also as co-educators of their children. The wide variety of opportunities available to the parents at Glenlee means that most parents can find something, whether a one-off event or a programme lasting six weeks, which meets their interests and encourages them to be involved. These include Rhyme Time (a programme from the National Literacy Trust), Storysacks, Play along Maths, Fit Start, Fit Food and Fit Futures (healthy eating programmes with recipes and challenges) and other literacy programmes such as the Adventures of Ted and Discovery Kits, summer family programmes and adult learning (South Lanarkshire Council, 2007, p. 12). The parents I spoke with during a field visit were particularly enthusiastic about a summer science programme. 'We were actually learning with them – it wasn't like a classroom – more like real life', said one parent. 'We talked about it for ages afterwards.'

Glenlee shares a campus with Hamilton School for the Deaf and for parents from both schools. An introductory sign language class for adults has been a great success. 'It has brought us closer together', agreed the parents who had attended the class, 'It wasn't about if your child was deaf or not, we all wanted to be able to communicate with the children and bring them in more.' The value of networks featured prominently in my discussions with the Glenlee parents. 'I have made new friends since coming to the group' was a frequent comment. Family learning programmes had brought them together and they found strength in sharing mutual concerns and learning from one another. 'Often you don't want to bother staff, but you can ask another parent things and they will know about it, and you can ask them things and not feel a fool – like how does this work and how would you do this.'

While there are many special opportunities for families to learn together, some are also woven into the day-by-day work of the school. During my visit one Primary 7 class was learning about genocide and the work of United Nations Children's Fund (UNICEF) in Darfur. They had written a proposal to their head teacher for permission to host a special event, at which they wanted to present their learning to their families. School staff commented on how working through the children was one of the most effective means of engaging with parents, whether through the family working together at home on a project, or whether through the parents being involved indirectly in a school activity. One teacher commented, 'Parents are really motivated to come along when their children are presenting – they are browbeaten by their children to attend, and the children are much better at doing that than we are!'

The partnership established with parents in Glenlee Primary establishes a sound basis for continuing the partnership into the associated high school. Programmes that are designed to help parents bridge the gap include 'Study Buddies', a science learning programme where families of children in Primary 7 can attend together an after school session and try out a range of scientific experiments, with challenges to be undertaken at home between sessions. The programme allows families to meet and make friends before their children start secondary in the autumn term. The strategic approach taken to home–school partnerships in South Lanarkshire means that the investment in primary continues seamlessly into secondary school.

Hill's Trust Primary, Glasgow: A parent-managed approach

By any measure, the breadth and depth of parental involvement supported in Hill's Trust Primary in Glasgow is remarkable. The school is situated in an area of Govan that ranks 23rd of over 6,000 of the most deprived small postcode areas in Scotland (Scottish Government, 2007c). In addition to the problems associated with poverty, the school faces the challenges of a diverse population, with many asylum seeking families and families of A8 nationals (that is, people from eight of the ten countries which acceded to the European Union in 2004, and who therefore have the right to live and work in the UK).

Born in 1995 of joint parent and teacher action to improve local play facilities and better parental involvement, the Hill's Trust Home School Community Project is a charity with a parent management group consisting of 12 enthusiastic parent members and one community representative. Its funding is mixed and insecure and it has only one full time worker. Yet is has an extensive and varied programme of activities in which families as a whole can become involved, including family events, holiday and seasonal activities. Becoming engaged in these activities has led in many cases to parents becoming engaged in learning for themselves. There are a large number of volunteer parents, who are recruited, trained, supported and celebrated. The Project is a successful combination of family support, family learning, parent volunteering and adult learning, with none of these functions adversely affecting the others because a common approach of respect and partnership underpins all of them. Those working for the project identify the main reasons for the success as committed school leadership over a long period, community management, good relationships with other agencies and the appointment of staff whose sole task is engaging with families. This last point raises an interesting dilemma for those who seek to promote family learning more widely. There are good arguments for appointing dedicated staff whose professional training prepares them for engaging with the most disengaged, and who are freed from other responsibilities (for example, classroom teaching) to devote time to working with families. This view is strongly supported by research commissioned by Save the Children (Sime and Duff, 2007). In some cases, the provision of additional staff can absolve teaching staff of the responsibility to attempt engagement. However, this is not the case in Hill's Trust; due to the commitment and leadership of the head teacher, the task of engaging with parents is regarded as everyone's business.

Bookstart: a community-based approach

Bookstart is a family literacy programme that has given a free pack of books to babies and guidance materials to parents and carers across the UK since 1992. Funded by the Book Trust, the public–private partnership has local co-ordinators who may be professionals from the health, libraries or Early Years Service. The impact of the programme is much wider than the gift of books, however. As an organisation, Bookstart not only promotes national events such as Bookstart Day, but also provides advice and support for reaching excluded groups such as the travelling community and makes special provision for hearing impaired children with its Bookshine Pack. It is also sensitive to the needs of a culturally diverse population. Bookstart has recently extended its programme to provide books at key stages of development: that is, 7 months, 18 months and 3 years, backed up by an online resource for parents (Bookstart, 2008). Research has demonstrated the positive influence of Bookstart in promoting increased family literacy. Longitudinal research on the impact of Bookstart demonstrates that the programme has not only led to an improvement of language and literacy performance upon school entry, but that Bookstart children maintain this advantage throughout their first five years of primary education. Mean scores for a range of literacy and numeracy tests showed Bookstart children outperforming their non-Bookstart counterparts by between 1 and 5 per cent (Wade and Moore, 2000, p. 31). Other studies have similarly demonstrated the long-term impact of Bookstart on attainment (Hines and Brooks, 2005).

Summary

Much good practice exists across Scotland, some of which is highly innovative and much of which can be demonstrated to lead to improved learning outcomes for both the children and the adults involved. Across a wide variety of school and community settings, there is an encouraging range of activity. Different methods are used, deriving from the different professional backgrounds of the staff involved. There is a growing interest in partnership working, which is leading to greater depth and provision in programmes. Moreover, there is clear evidence of the warm response of local families who find the approach accessible, rewarding and fun. Families who have once been engaged through well-designed programmes are likely to continue that engagement.

The extent to which professionals working with children and their families understand family learning as part of their core business is still not clear, however. There is a task to be done at a national level in identifying those professions for whom family learning is their sole business, those for whom it is a significant part, and those who have a smaller, but still important part to play. There is a clear need for national policy to define family learning as a key strategy in tackling underachievement. As long as national policy remains blind to the contribution of family learning, practice will continue to be patchy and vulnerable due to lack of funding.

CHAPTER 4

Family learning and social capital

> There is a strong case to be made for shifting the emphasis of our improvement efforts – and, by implication, our leadership practices in education – beyond an institutional or organisational focus, to one which acknowledges the relationship between the building of social capital in a networked context and its influence upon educational performance. *(West-Burnham and Otero, 2004, p. 3)*

Scotland has one of the most equitable and best performing education systems in the 30 member countries of the Organisation for Economic Co-operation and Development (OECD), reflecting Scotland's strong commitment to improvement in education. In spite of this accomplishment, the achievement gap is widening across the social class divide, as a disproportionate number of young people from lower socio-economic backgrounds leave school with only minimal qualifications (OECD, 2007). There is an increasing divergence between the growing achievements of the highest performing pupils in national exams and the static performance of the lowest performing 20 per cent. While recent improvements in Scottish schools have made a real difference for most pupils, they have failed to improve the education and therefore the life chances of a significant minority.

However, a number of schools have been successful in achieving improvements for all their pupils. Among the qualities that characterise these schools is partnership with parents and families. The others are high quality teaching, a strong commitment to inclusion and a positive ethos (HMIe, 2006a, p. 10). These findings are similar to findings in the USA, where positive home–school relations are identified among the characteristics of an effective school (Coleman, 1998, p. 81), and in England (Wolfendale and Bastiani, 2000, p. 2).

The challenge for schools to be successful for all their pupils lies not only in improving teaching, but also in taking a more inclusive, partnership approach to the communities they serve. This demands that schools look beyond the immediate presence of the pupils in their schools, and consider the family and community context of their work. It demands that schools think not just in terms of a flow of information out, but also of the inward flow. They must go beyond information sharing, in an effort to learn together. By working with others through a family learning approach, schools can play their part in reversing an otherwise downward spiral of underachievement, negative post-school outcomes, poverty and social exclusion (NAGCELL, 1998). Moreover, by collaborating with parents to build families as active communities of learners, schools can play a role in transforming the learning of their pupils (Coleman, 1998, p. 43) and in the creation of a learning society.

It is common to speak of some communities as 'deprived' and of some families as 'dysfunctional'. However, these views of communities and families may be blind to the cultural resource and the strength of connection enjoyed by those who live in them. Teachers who work in the schools which serve our poorest communities rarely live there, and may have little knowledge of the community beyond what they know of the children and parents in the school context. Interventions are introduced built on assumptions grounded in limited understanding of home and community contexts. There is rarely a lack of will to engage with the community, as teaching staff arc usually keen to engage, but may not always be certain how best to make productive connections. Schools may shelter behind their positional power through lack of direction and skill to engage effectively with families and communities. A study of how schools can facilitate the engagement of parents as partners in their children's learning found a great commitment to involving parents, but a lack of expertise in sharing with parents the ways in which they could support their children. Teachers may be committed to involving parents but not necessarily skilful at sharing information with them in ways that build productive relationships (Tett *et al.*, 2001, p. 56). Professional culture may apportion greater value to a professional body of knowledge than to less formal, less structured community-based learning.

◄REFLECTION▶

While employed as a home school project worker in the most deprived housing estate in Scotland, I took part in a job shadowing scheme in which teachers accompanied project workers on home visits. One afternoon I took a guidance teacher to meet a family I had been working with for some time. On the short drive to Stuart's home, the teacher expressed a sense of hopelessness about Stuart. Now in first year at secondary, Stuart could barely read, was not coping in Maths, and showed no interest in school learning. Stuart had missed a lot of schooling in primary, and the same pattern was beginning to emerge at secondary school. We were met in the home by Stuart and his mother. There followed a somewhat stilted conversation between the guidance teacher and the parent, while Stuart sat and sulked in the corner, aware his failings were the foremost issue in the minds of the two adults. As we rose to leave, I turned to Stuart and asked him if he would like to show his teacher his guinea pigs. Stuart took us into the room next door, which was filled from ceiling to floor with cages, all occupied by guinea pigs in a variety of sizes and colours. At first Stuart said little, but his guidance teacher skilfully asked questions about the animals, revealing that Stuart not only cared very well for the animals, but that he understood the basics of genetics, and was breeding the most popular colours and traits. He had a notebook recording his transactions with pet shops and other buyers, the costs of feeding the animals, the profit he was making and his plans for expansion. On his home ground, Stuart was not only a lad with a passion for his hobby, but a skilled, articulate and numerate entrepreneur. Moreover, he had extensive networks of people in his community with whom he shared his interest and who were supportive of his enterprise.

• •

Much of our public service has been unaware of or has ignored the value of community-based knowledge and networks and this is also true of schooling. School teachers have not traditionally been encouraged to be part of community networks, or to promote their development. They have not traditionally been interested in promoting an attribute that may be described as social capital. Social capital is not a new concept in schooling. Robert Putnam, in his exploration of what he regards as the increasing disconnection of individuals from their neighbours, communities and services in America, cites the first use of the term 'social capital' in 1916 by the then state supervisor of rural schools in West Virginia, L. J. Hanifan. Hanifan coined the term 'social capital' to describe the importance of community involvement for schools that wished to be successful. Hanifan defined social capital as, 'the tangible substances [that] count for most in the daily lives of people: namely good will, fellowship, sympathy, and social intercourse among the individuals and families who make up a social unit…'. He went on to explain:

> The individual is helpless socially, if left to himself. If he comes into contact with his neighbor, and they with other neighbors, there will be an accumulation of social capital, which may immediately satisfy his social needs and which may bear a social potentiality sufficient

to the substantial improvement of living conditions in the whole community. The community as a whole will benefit by the co-operation of all its parts, while the individual will find in his associations the advantages of the help, the sympathy, and the fellowship of his neighbors. (Putnam, 2000, p. 19)

Hanifan was responsible for the rural schools in West Virginia, and the role of the school in promoting social capital may have seemed more appropriate then than it does now, especially in more urban areas. Yet one common feature of all communities (except for the smallest and most remote) is the presence of a school. Many of our communities no longer have post offices or libraries. Village churches may be abandoned or poorly supported. In both rural settings and large urban housing estates, shops may be non-existent. Schools, however, especially nursery and primary schools, remain at the heart of most communities, and have the potential to serve as important hubs for community connection.

The expanding role of schools as promoters of social capital is beginning to receive some interest at a national level in UK. Current debates around school leadership are becoming concerned to define the type of leadership that is needed to take schools beyond the plateau that some believe they have reached in terms of improvement:

> There is a case for arguing that results at a national level have reached a plateau and significant improvements in attainment levels are increasingly difficult to secure ... In the education sector, attempts to tackle the issue of social poverty within the schooling system have historically been characterised by school improvement efforts. When schools concentrate their efforts internally on improving their own school or organisational system, this creates bonding, introspection and institutional integrity. However, it also leads to detachment and compromises engagement and networking – the very basis of social capital. On this basis alone, there is a strong case to be made for shifting the emphasis of our improvement efforts – and by implication our leadership practices in education – beyond an institutional or organisational focus, to one which acknowledges the relationship between the building of social capital in a networked context and its influence upon educational performance. (West-Burnham and Otero, 2004, p. 3)

We are accustomed to thinking of schools as having the purpose of developing intellectual capital. Increasingly we realise that they also need to develop social capital 'to help produce citizens who have the commitment, skills, and dispositions to foster norms of civility, compassion, fairness, trust, collaborative engagement and constructive critiques under conditions of great social diversity' (Fullan, 2003, p. 11). This realisation is evident in the purposes of the curriculum as defined in the Curriculum for Excellence. These are summed up as a set of aspirations for children and young people, that they should become 'successful learners', 'confident individuals', 'responsible citizens' and 'effective contributors' (Scottish Executive, 2004a).

The Applied Educational Research Scheme (AERS) was a Scottish consortium led by the universities of Edinburgh, Stirling and Strathclyde and funded by the Scottish Government Education Department and the Scottish Education Funding Council from 2004. AERS has been engaged in research into social capital and schools, evidencing an increasing interest in the topic north of the border. A key piece of learning to emerge is the distinction between 'productive' social capital and 'unproductive' social capital. By productive social capital AERS implies a social capital 'that can be developed, exchanged and recognised to make the school experience better, particularly for disadvantaged learners'. This is contrasted with an 'unproductive' social capital that bonds teaching staff by strengthening professional conservatism, rather than creating bridges – a phenomenon which the researchers found prevailed in the literature on teacher professionalism. They found that teacher socialisation was focused on technical competence to the exclusion of notions of inter-professionalism and collaboration with the community (Ozga *et al.*, 2008, p. 3).

In his study of educational change, Fullan suggests that the social, intellectual and professional isolation of teachers is rooted in pre-service training, where, in contrast to the professional preparation of other groups, there is little opportunity for students to collaborate in their learning (Fullan, 1993, p. 106). Much has changed with regard to teacher collaboration in Scotland in the last decade, however. Communities of practice/inquiry are developing in schools, particularly around curricular change. An example of this is the means by which formative assessment has been promoted. Under the heading Assessment is for Learning (AifL), schools were encouraged to bid for project funding to take forward developments in assessment. Learning and Teaching Scotland (LTS) defines an associated schools group (ASG) as:

any group of practitioners collaborating and working across traditional boundaries with the aim of developing professional practice. Groups vary in size and may consist of teachers working across classes or departments within a school or establishment, across a cluster of schools in an area, or even across authorities in a national context. (Learning and Teaching Scotland, 2008)

The ASGs became the power houses for AifL, contributing to what has become known as the 'quiet revolution' in classroom teaching, as teachers learned and shared together how to implement the new strategies (Learning and Teaching Scotland, 2008). In developing these networks, staff increased their social capital and became more outward looking and confident. Nor are examples of such networking dependent on national developments such as AifL. Brechin High School in Angus holds weekly 'learning lunches' attended by around a third of the teaching staff and focusing on issues in teaching and learning chosen by the staff (*Times Educational Supplement Scotland*, 21 November 2008).

While there has been an increasing trend towards teacher collaboration in continuing professional development in recent years, there are still many teachers in our schools who have experienced only didactic approaches in their own learning, and so struggle to adopt the more collaborative approaches demanded by curricular change and community involvement. The establishment of collaborative structures do not always guarantee that a culture of collaboration is developing (Fullan and Hargreaves, 1992). However, a recent study of the professional culture of teachers suggests that attitudes among newer entrants to the teaching profession in Scotland are more supportive of building social capital:

> Those who were still in their first two years of teaching tended to see the value of offering opportunities for pupils to influence change in school and negotiating some learning tasks and lesson content with pupils more than their other school colleagues. Teachers who had been in the profession for over twenty-four years were less appreciative of the role of parents in supporting learning. Similarly, they tended to disapprove of parents having a greater say in school decision-making. There was strong agreement from teachers who had been in the profession for less than ten years that schools should encourage local community involvement. (Hulme *et al.*, 2008, p. 34)

The value of a school staff collaborating with one another and becoming a professional learning community extends not only to practice within the school; the practice of being engaged together in learning makes teachers less defensive and more confident. They are not only more confident about working and learning with the community, they are also aware of how much better their practice becomes when they are no longer working on their own (Fullan, 2003, p. 44).

The AERS researchers propose some implications for policy in order to create more productive social capital in our schools. Such policies should promote:

- broader understandings of the principles of professionalism in the context of change and inter-professional working;
- stronger emphasis on understanding of, and engagement with the wider society in programmes of professional formation;
- more inter-professional training and development; and
- more attention to the positive aspects of diversity.

(Ozga *et al.*, 2008, p. 3)

HMIe has begun to associate the benefits of family learning with the strengthening of social capital (HMIe, 2008). In an investigation of the benefits of family learning in the early years, HMIe identified that the value of family learning practice may be seen beyond the immediate context of the family and can be found in the building of effective networks in the community. Adult participation in family learning was perceived to lead to the building of relationships, friendships and communities. Social contact extended through participation to people from different backgrounds, different minority ethnic groups and different ages.

The potential for family learning to promote productive social capital with the school acting as the network hub is as yet unrealised. The community schools initiative, launched by the Scottish Office in 1998, laid down some groundwork for the school as a community hub, but the aspects of community engagement and involvement were never as fully appreciated as intended in the original prospectus. The new community schools initiative expressed high ideals, but struggled to demonstrate its success due to a lack of workable success criteria. It became overshadowed by a narrow school improvement agenda and in particular the aspect of raising attainment. There were many notable achievements in developing the community engagement role for schools, but this was dependent on very personal local commitment. One of the overall successes of the venture, however, was its performance in acting as a catalyst for organisational change (Scottish Executive, 2002, p. 4; 2003, p. 12). Across Scotland, the notion of community development in schools was planted, and much of the current good practice in family learning is rooted in the new community schools programme.

Measuring the extent to which productive social capital has been achieved through schools is still in its infancy. Determining the extent of social capital presents challenges because most measures of social capital use instruments such as the number of people who vote, reflecting largely middle-class concerns. The AERS Social Capital in Schools Research programme has proposed instead the following indicators:

- community and family contacts with school;
- attitudes to school among communities and within families;
- school-related social activities among staff, and with community;
- friendship networks among staff, among students, and with communities;
- participation in school governance by staff, students, parents and communities;
- relationships with and among teachers and other school staff members;
- teachers' relationships with other professionals;
- communication and information within schools and with communities;
- responsiveness to particular issues, including diversity.

(Catts and Ozga, 2005, p. 4)

These indicators are largely determined from the school's perspective, and many of the issues mentioned – for example, participation in governance – may be divorced from the concerns of parents living with the more immediate concerns of poverty, disability and social exclusion. Interestingly, the indicator 'attitudes to school among communities and families' is listed, while the indicator 'attitudes to communities and families among schools' is not! As educators, our assumptions about where the responsibilities for change lies are so deeply rooted that we often betray ourselves by the perspective we take and the language we use. We assume that if the relationship between families and school are not as good as they might be, this is due to a need for attitude change at the community level, while ignoring school factors.

The argument I have been developing throughout the book is that family learning is based on three principles: that is, the recognition of the role of the family and community in a child's learning, the understanding of issues of power and language and the central role of dialogue in learning. On the basis of the arguments I propose instead the following indicators of social capital associated with family learning, along with practical measures for realising them. These indicators are sharing the vision, sharing the learning, sharing the access and sharing the achievements.

Sharing the vision

Descriptor: **School staff, pupils and parents come together to express interest and concerns and to find solutions to issues of mutual concern. In doing so, they share resources, learn from one another, bond together and build bridges between groups that previously may have been distant from one another.**

Sharing the vision can be accomplished through methods such as open space technology and appreciative enquiry. Open space technology was created by Harrison Owen as a method of holding meetings that fully engage a diverse group of people with minimum structure and a few simple, but important, rules (Owen, 1997, p. 10). Open space events release creative energy and help participants make powerful connections, sometimes with people with whom one previously had little in common. The act of coming together around one single identified issue, but with an open agenda, frees one from the normal constraints created by social status and diversity. Schools might, for example, invite pupils, parents and other members of the community to come together to spend two hours on a topic such as 'How to make our school better'. There are no assumptions as to what might make the school better, no hidden agenda and no preconceived answers. Nothing is ruled out or in. There is no leader, only a facilitator who helps the group to move forward in their discussion on matters of concern raised at the meeting. The topics for open space approaches are likely to be of local interest and concern, rather than issues imposed from above.

Appreciative Inquiry is a model of change management that can enable a school to engage its staff, parents and pupils in a joint effort to discover and to extend the school's strengths and advantages and to support bonding and networking that lead to positive change for the school. The key feature of Appreciative Inquiry is that it refuses to start from the position of a school's difficulties or problems; instead it focuses on its strengths. The model is based on the four 'D's: discovery, dream, design and destiny. The process takes those involved from *discovering* what is working well, *dreaming* about the school could be like if it worked from its strengths and *designing* the school to achieve the dream. In the first three phases, pupils, staff, parents and other stakeholders develop the networks and the creative co-operation that provide the springboard into the *destiny* phase, when the dream begins to be realised (Cooperrider and Whitney, 2005, p. 15).

Sharing the learning

Descriptor: **School staff and families experience learning opportunities to-gether on topics of mutual interest and concern, developing as 'communities of practice'.**

As discussed in Chapter 1, the notion of communities of practice is based on the work of Jean Lave and Etienne Wenger around social and situational learning. Wenger later applied the model to the world of education and organisational development (Wenger, 1998). According to Wenger, a community of practice will develop around an issue that is important to its members and will have three dimensions. It will be about a negotiated joint enterprise, it will function by a mutual engagement that binds members together in a social entity and it will develop over time a shared repertoire of feelings, routines, artefacts and vocabulary (Wenger 1998, p. 73).

Developing communities of practice between families, communities and schools can begin through the establishment of shared learning events. While social events can be useful in bringing members of the school community together in a more relaxed manner, shared learning events offer more potential for building social capital, while having the added benefit of focusing on the core purpose of the school. The *sharing* part of the event is the most important part. A teacher-run workshop on the curriculum is unlikely to be a shared learning event, because the teacher will assume in most cases the role of the expert, while parents are often seen as the recipients of knowledge. When teachers, pupils, parents and other stakeholders come together to share learning, synergy develops, considerably enhancing the learning that could be achieved if the groups were not working together. To create a shared learning event or task, a topic that is of interest to parents and pupils is identified. For example, a topic such as bullying is often of interest to everyone in a school community. As a school progresses and becomes more experienced and confident in shared learning, topics can become more advanced: for example, by learning about homework or learning about learning itself.

The key feature of a shared learning event is that everyone has something to contribute and something to learn. There may be an end product, such as a policy or a strategy, but it is the process which is important for building social capital. For example, a new homework policy may form part of the operational plan for a primary school. The school management team have planned to revise the policy because they are aware the existing policy gives teachers too little guidance and because the school is experiencing great difficulty in getting a large group of pupils to complete homework. Using a variety of methods – including small group discussions, open space, surveys – teachers, pupils and parents share concerns about homework and begin to define as a group what the purpose of homework is and how it can best be achieved. Pupils learn how teachers understand the purpose of homework, but more importantly, they learn that their teachers are open to new ideas, and believe they have something to learn from pupils and families. Parents feel more involved having been able to share their concerns about supporting their children. Teachers are clearer themselves about the purpose of homework, and how it might be set in a more productive fashion. The degree of consensus, commitment and new knowledge is well worth the effort expended. New networks and relationships have been established that will be of value for other purposes.

Sharing the access

Descriptor: **Activities and programmes for families are so designed that it is possible for all to take part, whether these take place at school, in the home or in the community. Special efforts are made to ensure that under-represented groups are successfully engaged.**

Inclusion is an essential component of any attempt to build productive social capital. Most school communities are diverse, and need to consider carefully how to include all the families of their pupils, regardless of ethnicity, gender, disability, sexual orientation and faith. One route into equality-proofing parental involvement and family learning activity is to consider the barriers families may face in becoming involved with their children's learning in its widest sense. It is common practice to ensure, for example, that the deaf parents of a hearing child has the services of an interpreter for a formal parents evening. However, it is less common to ensure that the same services are available for all family learning activities. A great deal of celebration and family activity takes place around schools at Christmas, but there are sometimes rather less opportunities for families of other faiths. Story reading and book lending are common practices in nurseries, but less common is the practice of telling stories and lending books in the languages used in the homes of children from minority ethnic groups.

The power of inclusion can be illustrated by the words of a profoundly deaf parent who is speaking through an interpreter about her experience of a family learning programme involving a group of parents and children working with a drama specialist to prepare and perform a circus event for other families:

> It was like a therapy for me. It's been marvellous. We started seven weeks ago. I really, really enjoyed it and especially having an interpreter there. That meant I was able to participate for the first time. I was really involved and on an equal footing with all the other hearing mothers, because I am the only deaf person in the group. When we were working with the children I felt very confident and I thoroughly enjoyed myself mixing with everyone in the hearing environment. I think it is great way that the family can get together. (East Renfrewshire Council, 2005)

Sharing the achievements

Descriptor: The whole school community celebrates learning together.

School events where achievements are shared and success is celebrated are normally well attended by families. Schools frequently report almost 100 per cent attendances for school concerts, plays, prize giving and graduations. Yet the achievements celebrated are normally rooted in school programmes and have little to do with learning within the family. In 2005, the Family Learning Service in East Renfrewshire held a special event celebrating family learning that has taken place over the previous year, bringing together over 50 families from different schools and communities to share together their successes, including the presentation of a family circus event prepared by families from one of the schools (East Renfrewshire Council, 2005). However, celebrating learning in the family need not be on such a large scale. Many schools have achievement boards or albums where the achievements of children both within and outwith the school can be celebrated and some schools invite families to use these to celebrate learning that has taken place within the family or community.

While Scottish schools continue to perform well in relation to other OECD countries, there is an increasing gap between the achievements of children and young people from different socio-economic backgrounds (OECD, 2007). There is an increasing recognition that school improvement may have peaked and that in order to improve further, more attention needs to be paid to building social capital (West-Burnham and Otero, 2004, p. 3). The emerging interest in social capital in Scotland provides an opportunity for schools and other services that provide family learning to be recognised as playing a critical role in promoting social capital. The theoretical understandings of social capital and the political imperatives driving them have created ideal conditions in which family learning can flourish.

CHAPTER 5

Evaluating family learning

Everything that can be counted does not necessarily count; everything that counts cannot necessarily be counted. (Albert Einstein)

Practice in promoting family learning varies across Scotland, taking place in different contexts, managed by a range of agencies and being informed by varied value systems. Not surprisingly, there is also a range of means of evaluating its effectiveness and little central direction. This chapter explores some of the evaluation that has taken place, suggests one means of extending the existing school evaluation tools to encompass family learning and presents a case study of using an appreciative inquiry approach.

Raising attainment

One of the most persuasive arguments for schools to adopt any initiative is that it can be demonstrated to raise attainment. One means of assessing the quality of family learning practice is to examine the extent to which it had played a part in achieving better learning outcomes. Robust evidence is beginning to appear that involvement in family learning activity has an impact on measurable outcomes for the children involved (HMIe, 2006b). Such evidence is vital to secure long-term funding for activities, and to demonstrate that actual transformation is taking place.

In 2006, Aberdeen City Council was recognised by HMIe for its good practice in family learning, as evidenced by the success of an innovative programme called 'Challenge Dads'. This project was successful in involving fathers in actively supporting their children's learning, but was also part of a much larger family learning operation that had demonstrated success in raising attainment. These included providing increased opportunities for parents and carers to become more involved in their children's formal learning; to become more aware and value their input in their children's learning; and providing learning opportunities for adults to improve their literacy and numeracy skills.

The HMIe report found that Challenge Dads and family learning were successful in developing the self-confidence of parents involved, in enriching their relationships with their children, and in supporting their progression to further education, training and employment. A range of innovative family learning projects had been established and these involved parents in actively supporting their children's learning. The Council was able to demonstrate that the children of parents who took part in family learning had made greater progress in language and maths than their peers whose parents were not involved in the family learning programmes (HMIe, 2006b, p. 8).

Family learning has a strategic position in Aberdeen City, forming as it does a crucial component of the Council's Community Learning and Development Strategy and the Adult Literacy and Numeracy Action Plan. It is also linked strategically with the Council's Early Years Strategy. Working across eight city schools that serve areas of deprivation, a Family Learning Team works with parents and carers of children aged between three and six years. Community Learning and Development staff in the Family Learning Team provide increased opportunities for parents and carers to become more involved in their children's learning; to become more aware of and value their own input in their children's learning; and to provide learning opportunities for adults to improve their own literacy and numeracy skills.

Aberdeen City Council had been collecting data on attainment using Performance Indicators in Primary Schools (PIPS), assessments of progress in Maths and Reading since 1997. PIPS is produced by the Centre for Evaluation and Monitoring at the University of Durham and enables participating schools to judge their performance within the context of the thousands of other schools that take part in the assessments. As part of this process of assessment in Aberdeen City, the scores of pupils in Primary 1 who had been involved in family learning activity in their pre-school years were compared with the scores of those who had not. Not only had children who had been involved in family learning started school with a significantly higher score than those who had not, but they had also maintained their lead at the end of Primary 1. These differences were apparent in two separate cohorts of young people starting and ending Primary 1 over a two-year period (Aberdeen City Council, 2008).

This example demonstrates what those who have been long involved in family learning have suspected, that the programmes make a measurable difference to attainment. There is now a challenge to practitioners to be more rigorous and routine in recording and tracking the attainment of the children involved in family learning programmes. For the same reason, there is a challenge to local authorities to recognise the potential of family learning to achieve hard outcomes, and to secure funding for these services.

Self-evaluation using quality indicators

The Scottish education system has received international recognition for its approach to quality improvement, combining self-evaluation and external evaluation, based on *How Good is Our School?* (HMIe, 1996, 2002 and 2007a). The self-evaluation approach uses a set of quality indicators to help users identify strengths and areas for improvement. Linked to strategic and operational school planning, it has provided schools with a very clear view of the expectations of government, and has helped government introduce new policies and procedures. Since its introduction in 1996, the *How Good is Our...?* approach has been extended to community learning and development, children's services and further education, and the guidance has been revised twice, the most recent version emerging in 2007, bringing the tool into line with the Excellence Model of the European Foundation of Quality. In the intervening years, a plethora of supporting documents were published by HMIe, asking 'How good is our school?' across a range of issues, including transitions, college partnerships, enterprise and health promotion (but not family learning). Critics of the approach have challenged the lack of explicit professional values (Lennon, 2008, p. 388) and its supposed inflexibility, which is seen as discouraging teachers from being innovative (Weir, 2008, p. 147). Nevertheless, there is little doubt (Christie and Kirkwood, 2006) that teachers' familiarity in using the self-evaluation approach has led to a more reflective profession, one which is accustomed to asking itself the key questions: that is, how are we doing, how do we know and what are we going to do now? It has also familiarised the profession with the notion of quality indicators, and suggested key questions that can be asked about each. The most recent version of *How Good is Our School?* is based on six key questions and these are mirrored in the version for community learning and development:

- What outcomes have we achieved?
- How well do we meet the needs of our school community?
- How good is the education we provide through the curriculum or learning and teaching?
- How good is our management in terms of planning, the use of resources or deployment of staff?
- How good is our leadership?
- How good can we be?

Exploring these questions in relationship to family learning can provide a good overview of how effective our family learning may be. Schools, community learning and development services and other organisations may find it helpful in using the framework to refer to the following illustrations of very good performance in family learning:

What key outcomes have we achieved?

A high proportion of the families of those children who are most at risk of missing out are engaged in our programmes: that is, they are not merely involved in being present, but are actively participating in both the delivery and the planning of activities. The children of families involved in our programmes demonstrate improvements in their attainments. Families who are engaged in our programmes are becoming more successful and confident. They exercise responsibility and contribute to the life of the school and the wider community. The priorities we have set for family learning in our school improvement plan have had a measurable impact by improving the engagement, achievements, attainment and well-being of families.

How well do we meet the needs of our school community and stakeholders?

We know our community well and appreciate its strengths, needs and diversity. We actively seek to engage the most vulnerable families in being involved in their children's learning and development. We make provision for families that experience most difficulty in becoming involved in their children's learning. We listen to what families share with us about their child's learning and development and take part in discussions about a child's learning with the child and the family. Families report that they feel more confident, better supported, more respected, more included and more involved in their children's learning.

How good is our delivery of key processes?

We provide easy access to a good range of family learning programmes that are lively, fun and varied to suit an assortment of different interests, needs and capacities. Programmes are designed in partnership with families and there is provision for progression into other forms of learning. We use high quality materials and make suitable accommodation available when required. We provide crèche facilities when required. Good relationships are developed between the families and those who provide the learning opportunities. Families are encouraged to see their progression in learning and to celebrate achievements. Families enjoy learning together and are highly motivated to continue learning in different contexts, but most especially in their own homes and communities.

How good is our management?

We have a clear framework for family learning that is based on local and school improvement plans, and which place family learning at the heart of what we do as a school or organisation. Family learning is not an *ad hoc* affair, but an important part of our core business. Resources for family learning are well designed for our community, and are stimulating to use, well organised and maintained. We take due regard for health and safety in all our family learning programmes, and all events are risk assessed. We gather data on the engagement of families, on their progression and achievements and we track the attainment and achievements of the children. We analyse the data to evaluate our progress and to plan for improvements.

How good is our leadership?

We have a clearly articulated vision for family learning that acknowledges the central role of the family in a child's learning, and regards family learning as an important part of our core business as a school or organisation. Our vision is apparent in our aims, values and in the way we conduct our day-to-day business. We strongly support equality by making every effort to engage the most vulnerable and most excluded families. We employ a strategic approach to family learning, prioritising tasks in line with our objectives. We are committed to partnership working, both with families and with other agencies who collaborate with us in delivering family learning. We are dedicated to improving our family learning services.

What is our capacity for improvement?

We have established a culture of self-evaluation that enables us to accurately assess our progress and to plan for improvement. In developing our family learning we have cultivated productive social capital and increased capacity by building relationships and expanding networks. We have established means of measuring our progress and producing evidence that our practice leads to the planned outcomes. We use a wide variety of means of consulting with families in order to ensure that we benefit from the views of families which might otherwise be seldom heard.

Evaluating family learning using participatory appraisal: a case study

Using quality indicators as an evaluation tool can give schools and other organisations that practice family learning not only an overview of progress, but also the opportunity to look in more detail at discrete areas, for example, leadership. It is important to involve participants in the evaluation process, especially those who may not wish to take part in a meeting, or fill in a questionnaire. Taking a closer look at our practices with participants is particularly important when new methods are being piloted and when we wish to understand at a deeper level the impact on participants.

Participatory appraisal, originally called participatory rural appraisal, developed in the early 1990s, when the approach was used as a means of engaging with rural communities in the developing world. It has since been extended and adapted for other issues: for example, health, literacy, education and urban development (Chambers, 1997, pp. 120–2). Participatory appraisal is based on the notion that professionals engaged in community development can be blind to the lived realities of the communities they seek to assist, and that the methods used to consult with communities can be inaccessible because they rely too greatly on technical details and on text. There is now a wide range of methods and techniques used in participatory appraisal that have been developed as the approach has been adopted in different contexts, but the common features are: use of visual material such as mapping, timelines and scaling; dialogue through interviews and focus groups; feedback to check for understanding and a continuing process of evaluation which informs the next step (Chambers, 1997, pp. 116–99). Unlike evaluation based on questionnaires, evaluation through participatory appraisal does not start with a set of predetermined questions – the questions evolve during the process.

Questionnaires, on the other hand, tend to select and simplify reality and to ask questions about the issue from an outsider's perspective.

There are three foundations to the process of participatory appraisal: behaviours, methods and partnership:

- behaviours: outsiders facilitate, not dominate;
- methods: methods shift the normal balance from closed to open, from individual to group, from verbal to visual, from measuring to comparing;
- partnership: sharing of information, experience, resources and training between insiders and outsiders, and between organizations. (Chambers, 1997, pp. 104–5)

Applying the participatory approach to family learning can result in parents being highly engaged with the evaluation, planning and managing of programmes. There is also a longer term impact on the workers concerned; participatory appraisal becomes not just a model of evaluation, but a mode of working in family learning.

In 2004, the Family Learning Service in East Renfrewshire was invited to take part in one of five national exemplar projects exploring how well-being could be fostered in a community. The exemplar projects were financed by the National Programme for Improving Mental Health and Well Being, and supported by the Scottish Development Centre for Mental Health (SDC) in collaboration with the Community Health Exchange (CHEX). The projects were diverse, but had a common theme, that of developing a sense of connectedness. They also had a common evaluation approach, devised by Niki Kandirikirira for the SDC, and the approach used was based on participatory appraisal (Kandirikirira, 2006, p. 10). Critical to the value of the exemplar projects was the extent to which they were able to demonstrate impact on individuals, relations, friends, peers and the community. They also needed to demonstrate improvements in relationships between people, (especially between individuals and organisations), changes in practice and multi-disciplinary co-operation. Each project used participatory approaches to assess impact in these areas, using a variety of means including maps, diaries, photographs, poetry and focus groups. The result was objectively verifiable evidence of the impact of the projects (Kandirikirira, 2006, p. 13).

The design of the East Renfrewshire exemplar project arose from the identification of mental health as an issue within the pilot new community schools initiative in a health needs assessment carried out by the Greater Glasgow

Health Board in 2000. The promotion of mental health in its widest sense became one of the major themes for the pilot schools, and it was good practice in this area that led to the SDC's interest in the work being done with families in the area and the award of exemplar project status. The project consisted of a number of smaller projects that operated in different schools, but had the common theme of developing a 'feel-good factor' in the families concerned. Activities were designed around the expressed interests of the families concerned and included classes for parents to explore the time parents need for themselves, family activities involving visual and performance arts, holiday activities and outings. The project staff modelled their values, beliefs and principles in the way they thought about the work, how they presented themselves and what they did. The project's direction, strategies, working styles, methods, decision-making patterns were all organised around these beliefs and principles (Kandirikirira, 2006, p. 10).

Central to the evaluation of the project was the use of photography. Images were collected of activities involving the families that participated. These images became the focus of open discussion with participants, reviewing and expressing what had happened during the programme, what they had felt and what it had meant for them. Qualitative statements were added to the images in speech bubbles. The implications and impact revealed in the statements were reviewed and verified with the participants. For example, a photograph of a group of children and parents at a drumming workshop was discussed with the participants and quotes from the discussion were used to further tease out what the impact had been. One mother had said, 'I would love to have one of these drums at home and in that way I would not need to be on anti-depressants and that would be great.' Considering the quote and the picture, the others agreed that the drumming event had helped with stress release by reducing isolation as participants were united through the combined sound of the drums. The participants also felt that the event had offered them choices that might signpost them towards other changes in their health and lifestyle. Similar processes identified the main benefits for the project as reducing stress, increasing the power of association, uniting people who had the same issues, and encouraging ownership and responsibility for the next steps in family learning.

These methods objectively verified that the project had had an impact on families by:

- supporting parenting;
- developing communities of practice (one group of parents so

valued the summer programme that they organised themselves and accessed training to run it for themselves the following year); and

- strengthening friendships and networks.

The project had also had an impact on social inclusion through:

- including parents with disabilities and those from minority ethnic groups.

The impact on community development was demonstrated through:

- a growth in self-sustaining groups and self-managed projects;
- stronger support systems; and
- intergenerational work.

Changes in practice had been an objective for all of the exemplar projects, but it was not possible to demonstrate significant impact in this area. Through reflection and discussion the proposition emerged that statutory services would have real difficulty in working in ways that would have facilitated such social change. Several reasons were identified for the lack of change, including organisational structure, procedures and power relations. Statutory services were regarded as being too rigid to respond to meet the needs of community processes in the way that family learning does. There is a limited tolerance in statutory service for experimentation and creativity (Kandirikirira, 2006, p. 15).

Summary

Evaluating family learning, in whatever context it operates and whatever form it takes, is crucial to making a strong argument to sustain projects and funding. Robust evaluation that provides both illustrative and comparative data is needed to indicate where practice is effective and where improvements are needed. Attainment data, self-evaluation and participatory approaches all have a part to play. Just as family learning needs to be embedded into statutory practice to ensure its future in transforming learning, the evaluation of family learning also needs to be embedded into the evaluation and planning for improvement systems of our schools and other agencies.

CHAPTER 6

Mainstreaming family learning

Scratch a good teacher and you will find a moral purpose.
(Fullan, 1993, p. 10)

Family learning involves families enjoying learning together. Those who seek to promote family learning acknowledge the central role of the family in a child's learning, validate the nature of that learning by engaging families in dialogue about learning, and facilitate the participation of families in the design and enjoyment of learning.

Having defined family learning in the above terms in Chapter 1, outlined its key principles, examined current practice, and having made suggestions for evaluation, I now turn to considering how family learning can become a mainstream approach. The mainstreaming of family learning offers opportunities to promote it universally, rather than exclusively in disadvantaged communities as at present. I have already argued in Chapter 1 that there are good reasons to consider it in a wider context, given the changing nature of the family in society.

Across Scotland, family learning that conforms to the above definition is a rare species, planted sparsely and flourishing only where local vision and commitment permits, whereas in England it is a much more established and accepted part of provision, supported by the Campaign for Learning and by the National Institute for Adult and Continuing Education (NIACE). As long as the promotion of family learning relies totally on the services of agencies external to the school, growth in family learning will be patchy and inconsistent, especially if limited resources are understandably devoted to issues of social inclusion. If Scotland is to reduce the gap significantly between the achievements of most children and that of the most disadvantaged, schools will have to become much more central to the task of promoting family learning than they are at present. For too long, too much of the limited investment in family learning has gone into short-term projects rather than building the capacity for delivery among the core universal services such as schools (Scottish Government, 2008, p. 17). Schools need now to be supported to develop fully their role in promoting family learning, a role that has three clear aspects. Firstly, schools have a role in acknowledging the home and community as contexts for learning. This implies respect for learning that is other than school learning and an acceptance that much valuable learning is taking place beyond the school's knowledge, and indeed beyond its gates. Secondly, schools have a part to play in validating that learning by accepting that it has a place in influencing what happens in school, and that it may sometimes change the way we approach the planning of our teaching and learning. Finally, schools need now to take some share in the responsibility for facilitating family learning in practical ways.

This requires a cultural change in schools, from organisations that work in isolation to centres of excellence in communication, collaboration and co-operation with their communities. Moreover, it requires changes in the way we train, support and resource school staff to work effectively with families. It challenges authorities to free teachers to rediscover what Fullan describes as their 'moral purpose', a purpose he suggests has been a casualty of excessive prescription over the past 20 years. Fullan envisages schools becoming 'engaged learning communities' where staff collaborate with each other and with the external world to better serve the moral purpose of schooling (Fullan, 2003, pp. 11–20).

It is worthwhile examining what lessons have been learned about influencing educational change, and to consider how these can be applied to family learning. Michael Fullan, in his study of the forces that lead to educational change, has identified eight basic lessons in managing educational change. Of these eight, four are particularly important to the topic of schools developing family learning. These are:

- You can't mandate what matters.
- Both top down and bottom up strategies are necessary.
- Connection with the wider environment is critical for success.
- Everyone can be a change agent. (Fullan, 1993, pp. 21–38)

Legislation can be a powerful means of forcing change, but it has its limitations where the change sought is complex. When the Scottish Schools (Parental Involvement) Act was introduced in 2006, it forced through a change that was unpopular with many schools and education authorities – the disbanding of

School Boards and the establishment of Parent Councils. However, when the Bill was first introduced a more complex and demanding change was desired by the Scottish Executive, as signalled by the introduction to the consultation on the Bill written by the then Minster for Education and Young People, Peter Peacock:

> All the evidence is that children do better when parents are actively involved in supporting and helping their child's learning. Parents who encourage their children to learn and actively support that learning will significantly improve their child's chances of success.
>
> This paper sets out our vision of how we can encourage and support parents more, both as individuals and as part of the wider school community. We want to achieve stronger, more inclusive and effective parental involvement in all aspects of education and a new partnership between parents and schools. (Scottish Executive, 2005, p. 1)

This vision was not possible to mandate, neither by the Act itself, nor by the accompanying Guidance. One of the problems about attempting to 'mandate what matters' is that product can win over process – instead of engaging with the process of supporting parents to be actively involved in their child's learning, the Executive became absorbed in producing a parent representative body, and the legislative requirements necessary to produce it. Innovation can become a goal in itself – a knee jerk reaction to the need for change. Structural change is easy, cultural change is hard. Structural change is linear and easily quantifiable. Cultural change is a challenge to quantify. At the political level, quick fixes that can demonstrate hard outcomes are often chosen in preference to fundamental changes that will not bear fruit in the lifetime of a parliament.

Although it is not possible to achieve cultural change by mandate, some top down developments are needed, as well as the bottom up approaches. As we saw in the case examples in Chapter 3, political will at local authority level to commit resources and provide strategic direction can result in a well-established service that is embedded in school culture and is therefore sustainable. Centralisation of services such as research and development in bodies such as AERS and Learning and Teaching Scotland can provide leadership at the national level to enable change at the local level. The example of health promoting schools in Scotland is instructive. Prior to 2002, when the Scottish Health Promoting Schools Unit (SHPSU) was established by a partnership between Learning and Teaching Scotland, the Convention of Scottish Local

Authorities and Health Scotland, the promoting of health within Scottish schools was patchy. There were no nationally accepted definitions, no agreed benchmarks and no clarity about the role of agencies in supporting schools to promote health. SHPSU was given the task of championing health promotion in schools. Within three years, the momentum that SHPSU created at a national level was mirrored by significant developments at a local level and a national accreditation had been introduced to endorse local accreditation schemes for health promoting schools. The notion of a champion for family learning came through very strongly in the Council survey on family learning which I carried out in 2008. Asked what would help, over 60 per cent of respondents responded with appeals for a national agency or champion to support the work of family learning.

Connection with the wider environment is critical to success, yet many schools still exist in a competitive environment, isolated not only from their communities, but also from other schools and agencies that could assist them in promoting family learning. Limited resources are better maximised when schools work with others. Collaborative enterprises increase creativity, as schools tap into other's ideas, as has increasingly been the case in learning communities and associated school groups. Fullan speaks of the need for the 'moral purpose' of the school being linked to the greater social good: for example, for the aims of the school to help every child to achieve their potential to be linked to the broader social aim of ending child poverty (Fullan, 1993, p. 38). School staff are understandably anxious about schools being seen as the panacea for all social ills, but this is less about finding new roles for teachers than finding new allies for teachers in an endeavour that already engages a much wider professional body.

Everyone can be a change agent in education, according to Fullan, for change is far too important to leave to experts. Systems may support change, but ultimately it is people that carry it out.

I therefore finally propose, below, how family learning can be promoted at all levels in Scottish education.

By central government –

- establishing a national agency to champion family learning;
- adopting and disseminating a definition of family learning and identifying the key partners who should be involved;
- committing financial resources to support family learning through local authorities;

- issuing practical guidelines through organisations such as Learning Teaching Scotland, Learning Connections, the Scottish Library and Information Council and HMIe;
- commissioning a programme of action research, case studies and the dissemination of good practice;
- discussing with the General Teaching Council for Scotland, the Standards Council for Community Learning and Development in Scotland and the higher education sector how best to develop skills and collaborative practice to support family learning amongst teachers and other professionals;
- establishing a quality framework for family learning.

By local government –

- reviewing the contribution to family learning that can be made by each of their departments and ensuring collaborative practices;
- working closely with representatives of the voluntary sector to promote family learning;
- identifying a specially designated team to devise a local strategy and operational plan to facilitate family learning;
- including clear proposals and targets for family learning in their local improvement plans.

By parents –

- having access to research evidence about the most effective types of parental involvement;
- being engaged more fully as partners in the learning process, rather than mere recipients of information and advice;
- being encouraged to share and to celebrate their experiences of supporting learning in the home and community.

By schools –

- planning family learning as a core function of the school;
- reviewing the contribution to family learning that can be made by each of their departments;
- reviewing homework policies and considering how current homework practices may be improved to better facilitate family learning;
- transforming parent evenings to become shared learning events;
- embedding objectives associated with family learning in strategic planning;

- measuring the outcomes from family learning activity.

By classroom teachers – .

- rediscovering moral purpose – if the task is about making a difference to the lives of children, then perhaps it is worth the extra effort;
- finding fellow travellers, among colleagues, pupils, parents and stakeholders;
- expanding knowledge of what works in family learning;
- building skills in family learning that can be applied at the classroom level.

———

It may seem odd to end a book about family learning, an approach which has traditionally been seen as community based, with an exhortation to classroom teachers. I do so, not to overload an already burdened profession, but to liberate it from what has so long diverted it from one of its core purposes. Family learning by its very nature is not and never can be the sole province of schools; however, in building powerful networks among teaching colleagues, parents, pupils and external agencies, schools can play a fuller part in promoting the family as a learning community, thus making a difference to the lives of the next generation. To borrow Fullan's words:

> The majority of people, I think, are growing weary of conflict in society, the widening gap of the haves and the have nots, the cold hand of technology, and other forms of impersonality and degradation of humanity. Instead, people have a deepening interior need to find and give meaning to life. There are few professions other than teaching where gaining personal meaning through improving the lives of others for years and generations to come is so palpable and profound. (Fullan, 1999, pp. 81–2)

References

Aberdeen City Council (2008) *The Impact of the Family Learning Team on Attainment in Schools in Aberdeen* (unpublished report)

Aitken, W. (2008) 'The local governance of education', in Bryce and Humes (2008), pp. 152–61

Alexander, T. (1996) 'Learning begins at home: implications for the learning society', in Bastiani, J. and Wolfendale, S. (eds) (1996) *Home–School Work in Britain*, London, David Fulton, pp. 15–27

Allsop, L. and Kyle, J. (1997) *Deaf Parents and Their Hearing Children*, Bristol: Deaf Studies Trust

Anderson, G. L. (1998) 'Towards authentic participation: deconstructing the discourses of participatory reforms in education', *American Educational Research Journal*, Vol. 35, pp. 571–603

Biggs, J. (1999) *Teaching for Quality Learning at University*, Buckingham: Open University Press

Bishop, S. (2008) *Running a Nurture Group*, London: Sage

Bookstart (2008) www.bookstart.org.uk (accessed 1 October 2008)

Bowlby, J. (1969) *Attachment and Loss: Attachment Vol. 1*, New York: Basic Books

Bruner, E. (1997) Socio-economic determinants of health: stress and the biology of inequality, *British Medical Journal*, 314, p. 1472

Bruner, J. (1977) *The Process of Education*, Cambridge, MA: Harvard University Press

Bruner, J. (1978) 'The role of dialogue in language acquisition', in Sinclair, A., Jarvelle, R. J. and Levelt, W. J. M. (eds) (1978) *The Child's Conception of Language*, New York: Springer-Verlag, pp. 28–35

Bryce, T. G. K. and Humes, W. M. (eds) (2008) *Scottish Education Third Edition: Beyond Devolution*, Edinburgh: Edinburgh University Press

Calderhead, J. (2006) 'Reflective teaching and teacher education', in Hartley, D. and Whitehead, M. (eds) (2006) *Teacher Education, Volume IV, Professionalism, Social Justice, and Teacher Education*, London: Taylor and Francis, pp. 35–47

Campaign for Learning (2008) *Overview* (online) Available from URL: www.campaign-for-learning.org.uk/cfl/fl/overview/index.asp (accessed 20 November 2008)

Catts, R. and Ozga, J. (2005) 'What Is Social Capital and How Might It Be Used in Scotland's Schools?' CES Briefing No. 36, University of Edinburgh, Centre for Educational Sociology (online). Available from URL: www.ces.ed.ac.uk/publications/briefings.htm (accessed 23 October 2008)

Chambers, R. (1997) *Whose Reality Counts? Putting the First Last*, Bourton-on-Dunsmore: ITDG

Christie, D. and Kirkwood, M. (2006) 'The new standards framework for Scottish teachers: facilitating or constraining reflective practice?' *Reflective Practice*, Vol. 7, No. 2, pp. 265–76

City of Glasgow (2009) Nurture Groups: A report to the Council (online). Available from URL: www.nurturegroups.org/data/files/downloads/glasgow_nurture_group_research_feb._2007.doc (accessed 8 May 2009)

Clouder, L. (2000) 'Reflective practice: realising its potential', *Physiotherapy*, Vol. 86, No. 10, pp. 517–22

Coleman, P. (1998) *Parent, Student and Teacher Collaboration: The Power of Three*, London: Sage

Cooperrider, D. L. and Whitney, D. (2005) *Appreciative Inquiry: A Positive Revolution in Change*, San Francisco: Berrett-Koehler

De Carvalho, M. E. (2001) *Rethinking Family–School Relations: A Critique of Parental Involvement in Schooling*, Philadelphia: Lawrence Erlbaum Associates

Department for Education and Employment (1997) *Excellence in Schools*, London: HMSO

Desforges, C. and Abouchaar A. (2003) *The Impact of Parental Involvement, Parental Support and Family Education on Pupil Achievements and Adjustment: A Literature Review*, Nottingham: Department for Education and Skills

Donaldson, M. (1978) *Children's Minds*, London: Fontana

Dyson, A. and Robson, E. (2002) *School, Family, Community: Mapping School Inclusion in the UK*, York: Joseph Rowntree Foundation

East Renfrewshire Council (2005) *Family Learning Celebrates* (unpublished transcript from DVD)

East Renfrewshire Council (2007) *Related to Learning: Engaging with Parents and Families, Promoting Parental Involvement: An Outline Strategy* (online). Available from URL: www.ea.e-renfrew.sch.uk/parents/documents/RelatedToLearningStrategy.pdf (accessed 16 May 2009)

East Renfrewshire Council (2008) *Adult and Family Learners: Your Life, Your Learning*, Barrhead: East Renfrewshire Council

Epstein, J. (2002) *School, Family, and Community Partnerships: Your Handbook for Action*, 2nd edn, Thousand Oaks, CA: Corwin Press

Freire, P. (1970) *The Pedagogy of the Oppressed*, Harmondsworth: Penguin

Fulcher, J. and Scott, J. (1999) *Sociology*, Oxford: Oxford University Press

Fullan, M. (1993) *Change Forces: Probing the Depths of Educational Reform*, London: Falmer Press

Fullan, M. (1999) *Change Forces: The Sequel*, London: Falmer Press

Fullan, M. (2003) *Change Forces with a Vengeance*, London: Falmer Press

Fullan, M. and Hargreaves, A. (1992) *What's Worth Fighting for in Your School?* Milton Keynes: Open University Press

Gillespie, J. (2008) 'The parent dimension in education', in Bryce and Humes (2008), pp. 193–202

Gorman, J. C. (2004) *Working with Parents of Students with Special Needs*, London: Corwin Press

Grant, D. (1989) *Learning Relations*, London: Routledge

Haggart, J. (2000) *Learning Legacies: A Guide to Family Learning*, Leicester: NIACE

Haggart, J. (2001) *Walking Ten Feet Tall: A Toolkit for Family Learning Practitioners*, Leicester: NIACE

Hanafin, J. and Lynch, A. (2002) 'Peripheral voices: parental involvement, social class, and educational disadvantage', *British Journal of Sociology of Education*, Vol. 23, No.1, pp. 35–49

Harris, J. R. (1998) *The Nurture Assumption: Why Children Turn Out the Way They Do*, New York: Simon and Schuster

Hines, M. and Brooks, G. (2005) *Sheffield Babies Love Books: An Evaluation of the Sheffield Bookstart Project*, Sheffield: University of Sheffield

HMIe (1996) *How Good is Our School?* Edinburgh: HMIe

HMIe (2002) *How Good is Our School? 2*, Edinburgh: HMIe

HMIe (2004) *Inspection of Adult Learning in East Renfrewshire Council*, Edinburgh: HMIe

HMIe (2006a) *Missing Out: A Report on Children at Risk of Missing Out on Educational Opportunities*, Edinburgh: HMIe

HMIe (2006b) *Community Learning and Development in the Seaton, Tillydrone and Woodside Areas* [of Aberdeen City], Edinburgh: HMIe

HMIe (2006c) *How Good is Our Community Learning and Development?* Edinburgh: HMIe

HMIe (2007) *How Good is Our School? The Journey to Excellence Part 3*, Edinburgh: HMIe

HMIe (2008) *Family Learning within the Early Years Framework* (online). Available from URL: www.scotland.gov.uk/Publications/2008/06/family-learning (accessed 20 September 2008)

Hulme, M., Elliot, D., McPhee, A. and Patrick, F. (2008) *Professional Culture among New Entrants to the Teaching Profession: Report to the General Teaching Council for Scotland and the Scottish Government*, Edinburgh: General Teaching Council for Scotland

Jones, J. and Macrae, C. (2008) *Scoping Study on Models of Family Learning*, Grangemouth: Linked Work and Training Trust

Juslin, P. W. and Bremberg, S. (2006) *Greater Parental Influence Enhances Educational Achievement: A Systematic Review* (online). Available from URL: www.fhi.se/upload/ar2006/Rapporter/r20063parentalinfluence0602.pdf (accessed 19 October 2008)

Kandirikirira, N. (2006) *Small Change, Big Impact: Building Community Well-Being: Can Scotland Afford Not To? Conference Report*, Edinburgh: Scottish Development Centre for Mental Health

Learning and Skills Council (2002) *Family Learning Supplementary Guidance 2002/03* (online). Available from URL: readingroom.lsc.gov.uk/pre2005/funding/streams/family-learning-supplementary-guidance.pdf (accessed 20 May 2009)

Learning and Teaching Scotland (2008) *About AifL – Assessment is for Learning* (online). Available from URL: www.ltscotland.org.uk/assess/about/index.asp (accessed 10 November 2008)

Learning and Teaching Scotland (2009) *Assessment and Achievement* (online). Available from URL: www.ltscotland.org.uk/curriculumforexcellence/assessmentandachievement/index.asp (accessed 10 June 2009)

Lennon, F. (2008) 'Organisation and management in the secondary school', in Bryce and Humes (2008), pp. 383–91

Lewis, A. and Forman, T. A. (2002) 'Contestation or collaboration? A comparative study of home–school relations', *Anthropology & Education Quarterly*, Vol. 33, No. l, pp. 60–89

Lochrie, M. (2004) *Family Learning: Building All Our Futures*, Leicester: NIACE

Loukes, N. (2004) *Prison without Bars: Needs, Support, and Good Practice for Work with Prisoners' Families* (online). Available from URL: www.familiesoutside.org.uk/downloads/contribute/PrisonWithoutBars.pdf (accessed 29 September 2008)

Loukes, N. (2006) *Evaluation of the Families United Pilot Programme at HMP Edinburgh* (online). Available from URL: www.therobertsontrust.org.uk/pubs/smile.pdf (accessed 29 September 2008)

Mackenzie, J. (2008) 'Disaffection with schooling', in Bryce and Humes (2008), pp. 762–71

Maclachlan, K. (1996) 'Good mothers are women too: the gender implications of parental involvement in education', in Bastiani, J. and Wolfendale, S. (eds) (1996) *Home–School Work in Britain*, London: David Fulton, pp. 28-38

McArdle, K. (2007) *A Research Report on the Role of the Scottish Network for Parental Involvement in Children's Learning*, Aberdeen: University of Aberdeen

McBeth, A. (1993) 'Preconceptions about parents in education', in Munn, P. (ed.) (1993) *Parents and Schools: Consumers, Managers or Partners?* London: Routledge, pp. 27-46

McGivney, V. (2000) *The Contribution of Pre-Schools to the Community: A Research Study on the Role of Pre-Schools in Combating Social Exclusion*, London: Pre-school Learning Alliance

Merriman, S. B., Caffarella, R. S. and Baumgartner, L. M. (2007) *Learning in Adulthood*, San Francisco, Jossey-Bass

Midlothian Council (2008) *An Evaluation of the Integration Teams in Midlothian Council* (unpublished report)

Moon, J. (1999) *Learning Journals: A Handbook for Academics, Students and Professional Development*, London: Kogan Page

Munn, P. (1993) *Parents and Schools: Customers, Managers or Partners?*, London: Routledge

NAGCELL (1998) *Learning for the Twenty-first Century*, London: NAGCELL

NIACE (2000) *A Manifesto for Family Learning*, London: NIACE

NIACE (2008) *Making the Connection: The Mental Health and Family Learning pack*, London: NIACE

Nurture Group Network (2008) www.nurturegroups.org (accessed 3 September 2008)

OECD (1997) *Parents as Partners in Schooling*, Paris: OECD

OECD (2007) *Reviews of National Policies for Education – Quality and Equity of Schooling in Scotland*, Paris: OECD

Orton, F. (1991) Linking Theory to Practice: The Experience of the Partnership in Education Project, Strathclyde, Scotland. Bernard van Leer Foundation Studies and Evaluation Papers No. 4. Education Resources Information Centre ED339540

Owen, H. (1997) *Open Space Technology, A User's Guide, 2nd Edn*, San Francisco: Berrett-Kohler Publishers

Ozga, J., Hulme, M. and McGonigal, J. (2008) *Teacher Professionalism and Social Capital: A Productive Relationship?* AERS Research Briefing Paper 2 (online). Available from URL: www.aers.org.uk (accessed 25 October 2008)

Putnam, R. D. (2000) *Bowling Alone: The Collapse and Revival of American Community*, New York: Simon and Schuster

Reading Agency (2008) www.readingagency.org.uk/adults/big-book-share/ (accessed 29 September 2008)

Roberts, P. (2000) *Education, Literacy, and Humanization: Exploring the Work of Paulo Freire*, Westport: Greenwood Publishing

Roberts, P. (2005) 'Pedagogy, politics and intellectual life: Freire in the age of the market', Policy Futures in Education, Vol. 3, No. 4, pp. 446–58

Scotland's Commissioner for Children and Young People (2008) *Not Seen, Not Heard, Not Guilty: The Rights and Status of Children of Prisoners in Scotland*, Edinburgh: SCCYP

Scottish Executive (1998) *New Community Schools Prospectus*, Edinburgh: Scottish Executive

Scottish Executive (2001) *A Teaching Profession for the 21st Century*, Edinburgh: Scottish Executive

Scottish Executive (2002) *National Evaluation of the New Community Schools Pilot Programme in Scotland: Phase 1: Interim Findings*, Edinburgh: Scottish Executive

Scottish Executive (2003) *Insight 7: Key Findings from the National Evaluation of the New Community Schools Pilot Programme in Scotland*, Edinburgh: Scottish Executive

Scottish Executive (2004a) *A Curriculum for Excellence*, Edinburgh: Scottish Executive

Scottish Executive (2004b) *Working and Learning Together to Build Stronger communities: Scottish Executive Guidance for Community Learning and Development*, Edinburgh: Scottish Executive

Scottish Executive (2005) *Making the Difference – Improving Parents' Involvement in Schools: A Consultation on a Draft Bill*, Edinburgh: Scottish Executive

Scottish Executive (2006a) *Guidance to the Scottish Schools (Parental Involvement) Act 2006*, Edinburgh: Scottish Executive

Scottish Executive (2006b) Scottish Schools (Parental Involvement) Act, Edinburgh: Scottish Executive

Scottish Executive (2006c) *Making the Difference, Practical Advice for Parents on Personal Learning Planning*, Edinburgh: Scottish Executive

Scottish Government (2007a) *Concordat between the Scottish Government and Local Government*, Edinburgh: Scottish Government

Scottish Government (2007b) *LEAP: A Manual for Learning Evaluation and Planning*, Edinburgh: Scottish Government

Scottish Government (2007c) *Index of Multiple Deprivation* (online). Available from URL: www.scotland.gov.uk/Topics/Statistics/SIMD/ (accessed 22 January 2009)

Scottish Government (2008) *Early Years Framework Part 1*, Edinburgh: Scottish Government

Scottish Office (1998) *New Community Schools Prospectus*, Edinburgh: Scottish Office

Sime, D. and Duff, E. (2007) *Improving Educational Outcomes for Children Living in Poverty through Parental Involvement in Primary Schools*, Edinburgh: Save the Children

Smith, M. K. (1999) 'Learning theory', *The Encyclopaedia of Informal Education* (online). Available from URL: www.infed.org/biblio/b-learn.htm (accessed 28 December 2007)

South Lanarkshire Council (2007) Home School Partnership Annual Review

Storms, M. D. (1997) 'Attribution theory, basic issues and applications', in Hewstone, M., Manstead, A. S. R. and Stroebe, W. (eds) (1997) *The Blackwell Reader in Social Psychology*, London: Wiley-Blackwell, pp. 172–88

Tett, L., Crowther, J. and O'Hara, P. (2000) 'Parents and schools' partnerships in early primary education', *Scottish Educational Review*, Vol. 33, No. 1, pp. 48–58

Thornton, S. (2002) *Growing Minds: An Introduction to Cognitive Development*, Basingstoke: Palgrave Macmillan

Tizard, B. (1975) *Early Childhood Education: A Review of Discussion of Research in Britain*, Windsor: National Foundation for Educational Research

Tizard, B. and Hughes, M. (2002) *Young Children Learning, Talking and Thinking at Home and at School,* 2nd edn, Oxford: Blackwell

Vincent, C. (1996) *Parents and Teachers: Power and Participation*, London: Falmer Press

Vincent, C. and Warren, S. (1998) 'Becoming a better parent? Motherhood, education and transition', *British Journal of Sociology of Education*, Vol. 19, No. 2, pp. 177–93

Wade, B. and Moore, M. (2000) 'A sure start with books', *Early Years*, Vol. 20, No. 2, pp. 3–46

Weir, D. (2008) 'Her Majesty's Inspectorate of Education (HMIe)', in Bryce and Humes (2008), pp. 142–51

Wenger, E. (1998) *Communities of Practice: Learning, Meaning and Identity*, Cambridge: Cambridge University Press

West-Burnham, J. and Otero, G. (2004) *What Are We Learning About? Leading Together to Build Social Capital*, Nottingham: National College for School Leadership

Wolfendale, S. and Bastiani, J. (2000) *The Contribution of Parents to School Effectiveness: Home and School, A Working Alliance*, Abingdon: David Fulton

INDEX